Praise for

I BELONG TO VIENNA

"An intimate account of a courageous family whose rich life in Vienna unravels into a struggle for survival. A suspenseful story of bravery, dignity, and the love of a city that withstands its bleakest chapter."

—ANNE-MARIE O'CONNOR,
author of *The Lady In Gold: The Extraordinary Tale of Gustav Klimt's Masterpiece, Portrait of Adele Bloch-Bauer*

"Why would you return to a city that tried to murder you? Here is the story of one Jewish family that did . . . Blends history, biography, and memoir . . . Well-researched, intimate, evocative look at some of the 20th century's foulest days."

—*KIRKUS REVIEWS*

"A meticulous evocation of an unknown Austria, Anna Goldenberg's affecting family memoir brings to life the story of Viennese Jews who decided not to flee their homes after the Anschluss. This salutary tribute forces us to reflect on what it means to try and live a 'normal life' in the throes of a political nightmare."

—GEORGE PROCHNIK,
author of *The Impossible Exile* and *Stranger in a Strange Land*

"A must-read for a new understanding of the Holocaust in Vienna and why a Jewish family would not let itself be uprooted despite the city's dark past."

—ESTHER SAFRAN FOER,
author of *I Want You to Know We're Still Here:*
A Post-Holocaust Memoir

"Anna Goldenberg brings the memory of her grandparents to life and sweeps us away with her portrayal of bravery and endurance. This is an important and wonderful book."

—DORON RABINOVICI,
author of *Elsewhere and The Search for M*

"Goldenberg has written a big, important, quiet and disturbing book. It is ruthless and precise, honest and inquisitive, showing the bright side of a family's fate as well as the dark."

—*FALTER*

"A kaleidoscopic picture of the varied perceptions of the oncoming Holocaust and how the Jewish population of Vienna responded to its events and risks."

—*DIE ZEIT*

"Goldenberg reveals the mechanisms by which people were initially deprived of their rights, then their property, and finally their lives—the processes necessary for dehumanization."

—*DER STANDARD*

I BELONG TO VIENNA

A JEWISH FAMILY'S STORY
OF EXILE AND RETURN

ANNA
GOLDENBERG

Translated from the German by Alta L. Price

NEW VESSEL PRESS
NEW YORK

New Vessel Press

www.newvesselpress.com

First published in German in 2018 as *Versteckte Jahre: Der Mann, der meinen Großvater rettete*

Copyright © 2018 Paul Zsolnay Verlag Ges.m.b.H.,Wien

Translation copyright © 2020 Alta L. Price

Published with support for the translation from the Federal Chancellery, Republic of Austria

Library of Congress Cataloging-in-Publication Data
Goldenberg, Anna
[Versteckte Jahre, English]
I Belong to Vienna: A Jewish Family's Story of Exile and Return / Anna Goldenberg;
translation by Alta L. Price.
p. cm.
ISBN 978-1-939931-84-9
Library of Congress Control Number 2019955324
I. Austria—Nonfiction

For Laura, Joni, Dylan, Beni, Adam,
Nunu, Luc, Gina, Ella, and Rafi

CONTENTS

FAMILY TREE

HANSI'S FAMILY

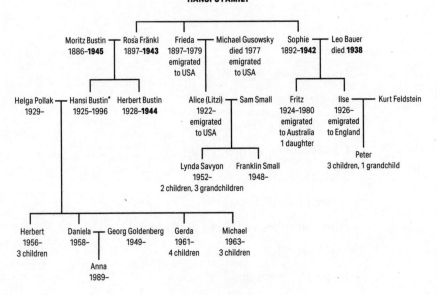

HELGA'S FAMILY

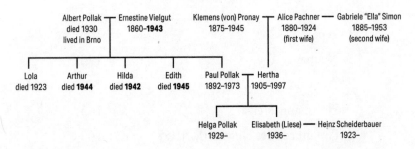

* Hansi Bustin was adopted by Josef "Pepi" Feldner in 1950 and changed his name to Feldner-Bustin.
BOLD date denotes killed in the Holocaust.

POUGHKEEPSIE, NEW YORK, 2013

"No photos." The broad-shouldered security guard in a dark blue jacket sounds firm yet polite as he gives me the once-over. I am so focused on taking a picture of the hospital's entrance hall that I didn't even notice him approaching. I'm in Poughkeepsie, in the Hudson Valley, north of New York City. A few people are waiting on benches, and the wall behind the reception desk—an oblong, mint-green counter—is painted brick red. The main glass door whirs when it opens. I lower my smartphone, which I had pointed toward the huge window overlooking the parking lot, and put it in my coat pocket, a bit intimidated. The guard turns away, visibly reassured to have warded off a threat. I summon the courage to ask him: is there anyone who might help me locate some old personnel files? He seems puzzled, thinks for a second, and leads me to the virtually empty hospital library, where I'm enthusiastically greeted by a librarian.

Back in the fifties, two young doctors from Vienna worked at this hospital, I tell her. They were interns—what we'd call residents today—and spent a year serving various departments. I'm now looking for documents, references, maybe old rosters—anything that might tell me more about their time here. The librarian replies that she'll gladly look into it, visibly flattered by the provincial hospital's international reputation. "What are their names?" "Helga and Hans Feldner-Bustin." She disappears into a back room. Five minutes later, she's back. No, unfortunately, they aren't in any of the old files. I'm so clearly disappointed that she asks why I'm interested. "They're my grandparents."

That evening I take the train some ninety miles back to New York City, downcast that no one here remembers my grandparents. After all, my grandmother Helga spoke of their stay here so often. In her bedroom there's even a newspaper clipping from 1955 hanging on the wall, from a Jewish-American newspaper. The photo shows a smiling young couple; Helga is twenty-six, Hansi twenty-nine. "Also aboard the *Saturnia* were Drs. Hans and Helga Feldner-Busztin [*sic*], who came from Vienna to intern at Poughkeepsie Hospital. Dr. Helga was liberated from Nazi concentration camp in 1945. Dr. Hans said his brother and parents perished in concentration camp but he escaped when a Christian doctor adopted him."

The two had arrived in the States still fairly undecided. They knew they'd definitely stay there a year, they said, and then they could see how they liked it. Due to the shortage of doctors in the United States, Helga was immediately given demanding work in Poughkeepsie, unlike the Viennese hospital where she had worked as an assistant doctor for the previous two and a half years. The salary was good too. Hansi had previously been an unpaid visiting physician at a neurological clinic in Vienna and had only earned pay for overnight services. In Poughkeepsie they could even afford a car,

A so aboard the Saturnia were Drs. Hans and Helga
Feldner-Busztin, who came from Vienna to interne at Poughkeepsie Hospital. Dr. Helga was liberated from Nazi concentration camp in 1945. Dr. Hans said his brother and parents
perished in concentration camp but he escaped when a Christian
doctor adopted him.

Helga and Hansi, 1950s.

which they shared with two other doctors. And yet by April 1956 they had gone back to Vienna, where they spent the rest of their lives.

I only began to wonder why when I moved to the United States myself. In the summer of 2012, I started my master's degree in New York City. I was 23, just a bit younger than my grandmother had been back then. New York had fascinated me since my teenage years, of course, because it had been the backdrop for pivotal scenes in so many movies. Here, Woody Allen had been funny in a way I had long enjoyed. Here, shy Spiderman saved people from all sorts of villains. Here, despite all adversities, the heroes of the rom-coms I adored invariably found each other.

With its various neighborhoods, cultures, and broad range of possibilities, the city was so visibly diverse that I was convinced I could make a place for myself here. Like my grandparents, I'd stay for a year and then see how I liked it.

Within the first few weeks of my arrival, though, I realized I was often misunderstood when I told people where I came from, especially when talking to local Jews. Many who heard my accent and learned I was Austrian became suspicious at first. "I'm Jewish," I said, as if to reassure them my ancestors hadn't committed war crimes. They were astonished: What? There are still Jews in Austria? Had my grandparents migrated from the Soviet Union after the war? No, I explained, my grandparents are Holocaust survivors who remained in their birthplace, Vienna, after the war. This was met with even more incomprehension. How could they live in a country where they'd been treated so terribly? Every now and then people's reactions sounded reproachful, as if my grandparents had lacked the pride or courage to leave Austria. "Many stayed for financial reasons," somebody once explained to me, with a condescending tone.

I had never made a big deal about my homeland. Like every member of a minority probably does, I often felt ignored. Why was there a Christmas break, even though I didn't celebrate the holiday? I didn't feel particularly Austrian. Still, it made me angry that my grandparents' decisions were being called into question. Did that mean something about my childhood and youth in Vienna was wrong, since it arose from my grandparents' questionable decision? At the same time, I myself had no adequate answers to such questions. That irked me even more. In fact, I couldn't quite understand why my grandparents had returned to Vienna. How had they found reconciliation with Austria? Weren't they constantly reminded of the humiliations they'd been subjected to following Hitler's 1938 annexation of their homeland?

The longer I lived in New York, far from my familiar surroundings, the more interested I became in my family history. In the winter of 2012, I participated in a radio reporting workshop as part of my master's program at the Columbia University Journalism School, and I called my grandmother Helga in Vienna. "What was your first impression of America?" I asked. "There was enough to eat," she replied.

A couple of weeks later, one cold, sunny January day in 2013, I go to Poughkeepsie: I wanted to see the America my grandparents had come to, to try out. The formerly industrial city lies right on the Hudson, a river spanned by numerous bridges. I see colorful, three-story homes with manicured front yards, lush lawns, and Victorian estates. It's a college town, so students now make up much of the population. It feels like a sweet, sleepy little place.

A few months later, my mother casually mentions the existence of Hansi's papers. Her father, my grandfather, died in 1996, when I was seven. I remember his black hair and bushy eyebrows. He kept his reading glasses on a strap around his neck, so they often lay on his stomach; Helga always found his belly too big, but he affectionately referred to it as his *Backhendlfriedhof*, a "cemetery" for classic Viennese fried chicken. When he was listening or deep in thought, he'd put his thumb and forefinger beside his nostrils and trace the wrinkles to the left and right of his upper lip, down around the corners of his mouth, until his fingers met again at his chin. I was sure that he'd inflicted the two furrows on himself with that tic.

I find over a hundred different text files in the folder my mother sends me. Hansi had begun to write about his life around 1986. Perhaps the uproar surrounding President Kurt Waldheim's wartime past, which sparked discussion of Austria's complicity in the Holocaust, prompted him to document his experiences. Maybe he was just trying out his first personal computer. He had visited the IBM factory in Poughkeepsie—describing it as "the company that produces electronic brains"—and enthusiastically written home that "an industrial revolution is underway here that's virtually unknown [in Austria]." Computers had fascinated him ever since.

Weeks go by before I look at his files. I want to establish myself as a journalist and deal with the fast-paced here and now—not the past, which we've already heard so much about. Besides, I already know a lot of Hansi's stories, since they're often retold within our family.

Finally, I read them.

MY GRANDFATHER'S PAPERS

Hansi doesn't write much about his childhood. He mainly describes his youthful transgressions since school hardly interested him. In 1931, barely six years old, he went to the elementary school on Kleine Sperlgasse in Vienna's second district. He got bad grades from the very start. It wasn't for lack of intelligence, teachers lamented, but rather his defiance and refusal to bow to authority. When he felt attacked, he quickly became angry. He wanted freedom—to play soccer, clamber over fences, and explore the narrow side streets, hidden courtyards, and nearby park, the Viennese Prater. On one foray he ended up at the children's outdoor pool at Franz-Josefs-Kai, but only after it had closed for the day. He was sent to juvenile court and got away without punishment. Another time he was caught playing soccer in a park where it wasn't allowed and his parents had to pick him up at the police station.

Hansi insists he wasn't rebelling against his parents; he just liked testing limits. He knew the family would never deprive him of its close affection and love: "They scolded and thundered at us, but we could always count on them, and always knew the family had a safety net ready to catch us."

Hansi's parents, Rosa and Moritz Bustin, ran a furniture shop on Margaretenstrasse in the fifth district. It was Rosa's

Hansi and his parents, Moritz and Rosa Bustin, circa 1930.

dowry. Moritz—who came from a German-speaking family in Uherský Brod, Moravia, and then moved to Vienna after serving on the front during World War I—oversaw the daily operations. Hansi's papers don't say how his parents met. On October 18, 1925, the day he was born, Rosa and Moritz had already been married for two years. And in January 1928 they had a second child, Herbert.

Hansi describes his father as charming, poised, and cheerful. He always had a well-groomed mustache. Hansi inherited not only Moritz's narrow face, black hair and eyes, and Mediterranean-looking olive skin, but also a love of good craftsmanship. My great-grandfather enjoyed working in the shop—he was handy and did many repairs himself. His hobbies included soccer and photography. He documented family trips to the Vienna Woods, their summer vacations in Bad Vöslau, their two sons playing in the courtyard. Sometimes he took Hansi to international soccer tournaments.

My great-grandmother Rosa was intelligent and engaged, read books, and went to concerts. There were times she hardly spoke, grew introspective, reflective, and a little sad. "My mother had the brains in the family," Hansi writes. "She could always see things clearly." Was it a happy marriage? Hansi notes that his father often wasn't there during summer vacation. Under the pretense of having to tend to the family business, he supposedly had a few affairs. Hansi only heard this many years later, from distant relatives. Was it true? We can't be certain.

Things felt harmonious on the home front, in any case, says Hansi, and his parents didn't argue in front of the children. He suspects his mother never knew of her husband's philandering, but can't be sure: "As a child, you can't really know your parents," he surmises.

The furniture business was brisk enough that the family could afford a large apartment in the second district, near the city center. Wandering in search of the address on a short, one-way lane called Schöllerhofgasse, I get a bit lost. It parallels Taborstrasse, and I'm amazed how close it is to places I know well. It's right near the subway station at Schwedenplatz, a spot bustling with people at all hours. It's also close to the Danube Canal and the waterfront promenade where I often take walks and go jogging. At one end of the lane lies a residential complex built in the 1960s; before that, it had housed the two-story Biedermeier apartment building where my grandfather grew up.

This reminds me of a story my aunt once told me: in 1966, when she was a teenager, she drove to the airport with her father—my grandfather, Hansi—to pick up a friend. My aunt was sitting in the back seat of the car, with a cast on her leg and crutches at her side. Another driver cut them off on the highway, whereupon Hansi followed him to the airport, got out, grabbed one of the crutches, and held it like a baseball bat as he threateningly went over to the other vehicle. The driver was so intimidated that Hansi's anger disappeared as quickly as it had come. I look at the place he grew up, in a building long since demolished, and try to reconcile this anecdote with the kind grandfather I remember from my childhood. I wonder whether I even knew my grandfather in the slightest—or will ever be able to understand who he was.

In the apartment in the building that doesn't exist anymore, there was a bathroom with running water and a tall copper boiler—both rare novelties for the twenties. Hansi and his brother, Herbert, played soccer in the spacious anteroom—because the floor below housed a grain company warehouse, nobody complained about noise. The family had a cook as well as a nanny to look after Hansi and Herbert. The division of labor wasn't without conflict. It seems the cook had a soft spot for the two boys, or she just wanted to make life difficult for the nanny: "There was constant bickering over the scope of their duties, which we kids really enjoyed," Hansi writes.

The family stayed in close contact with Rosa's two sisters. Rosa, Hansi's mother, was born in Vienna and had lost her mother when she and Frieda, her identical twin sister, were thirteen. Their eighteen-year-old sister, Sophie, then the oldest woman in the house, felt responsible for her siblings. Their father—who had left Poland for Vienna as a teenager, spoke German with a Viennese dialect, and had achieved a middle-class lifestyle through the furniture business—soon remarried. The three sisters' aversion to their stepmother brought them even closer together.

Just like Rosa's, Sophie and Frieda's dowries also included one of their father's furniture shops. Both were located on side streets off Landstrasser Hauptstrasse, the main commercial thoroughfare in the third district, near the city center. The sisters bore children in short order: Frieda's daughter was three years older, Sophie's son two years older, and her daughter nine months younger than Hansi. Five children in all, and they grew up like siblings.

Every Sunday the whole family gathered at Aunt Sophie's—naturally, as the eldest of the three sisters, she served as the hostess. They ate lunch, and then the men played rummy, sometimes in the living room, sometimes in one of the nearby coffeehouses. The sisters talked, the children played. If it was nice out, they'd go on day trips. Even during school vacations, most of the family went away together.

As I read Hansi's memories of his childhood, I was struck by how similar they were to my own. I was nearly always with my cousins, and often went home only to sleep. In all, there are eleven of us grandchildren, eight of whom grew up in Vienna. Over time the rest of the family also moved into apartments in the nineteenth-century building where my grandparents had settled in the sixties. My parents and I lived one block away. I even had my own room in my grandparents' place, where I did my homework when my parents were at work. Every evening at half past six, we had dinner. Rarely were there fewer than eight people seated around my aunt's dining table. The house was almost never quiet.

Of course it's no coincidence there are so many parallels between Hansi's childhood and mine. Close-knit family life was important to him, and he seldom missed being home for dinner. He always sat at the same head of the table. After each meal he'd push the tablecloth to one side and open a small drawer built into the table. It held his heartburn pills. As my grandmother gave him a stern stare and explained that, yet again, he'd eaten too much, too fast, he'd put a capsule in his mouth and wash it down with water.

When I got to New York, I realized I wasn't used to eating alone. At first I found it liberating. I was always on the go anyway, so I ate bagels on the subway, sushi on park benches, and ready-made salads from the supermarket while typing on my laptop in my university's lobby. It was pretty different from sitting at a family dinner in Vienna and listening to my relatives' daily banter. But the novelty soon wore off. No, I didn't want to go back to Vienna, but I missed our family dinners. Why wasn't there some high-tech way to beam me to the family dinner table for a few hours, and then spit me back out onto the streets of Manhattan?

Hansi (left) and Herbert

CHILDHOOD IN VIENNA: HANSI

In all the old snapshots, Hansi looks like a cheeky child—dark hair, slender face, lanky figure. He's always looking out of the corner of his eye, a bit scornfully, and seems to be sizing up whoever is looking at him. In one such photo, he's about six years old, and his little brother, Herbert, who's maybe three or four, has hooked arms with him. Both wear short lederhosen with embroidered suspenders and flaps, and white shirts underneath. A tuft of hair partially covers Hansi's eyebrows, and there's a piece of wood in the corner of his mouth that looks like a pipe. His posture is upright and confident. Herbert gazes at the camera, a little uncertain.

This isn't the only family photo where everyone is dressed in traditional garb. I find it a bit shocking at first. I had always refused to wear such clothes. For me, those costumes signified an identity I wasn't comfortable with. Too much pride in one's own roots—something you can take no credit for, nor do anything about—and a whole bunch of conservative ideas. The term *Lederhosene* ("lederhosen-wearers") was a synonym for the illegal Nazis of the 1930s, and traditional costume festivals were one of their preferred meeting places. When I discover the photo of Hansi and Herbert, I read up on it. Back then, for many people—even urban Jews like my family—it was normal to dress up this way for trips to the countryside, I learn. Those who could afford it went on summer vacation, and in the region between Semmering and the Salzkammergut, those who wanted to belong wore the local garb. Just how deeply entwined these clothes were with a particular identity becomes clear when you consider that on July 6, 1938, Jews were forbidden to wear national costumes "to avert the endangerment of public safety" because it threatened "to provoke legitimate indignation among the German population."

A few months after I first read that fact, in the summer of 2016, a folk festival takes place in my neighborhood. I usually avoid crowded events. I'm not exactly tall and don't like being jostled around, so I usually let others go on ahead and struggle to make my way through the hordes. But now I've recently moved back to Vienna, and some old schoolmates I'm still friends with want to go. Wearing dirndls. Am I in? All of a sudden, I realize I don't have to feel any hesitation anymore. Hansi liked wearing lederhosen his entire life, mostly on weekends, when he puttered around the house with his toolbox making minor repairs—a dripping tap here, a loose hinge there. Clothing is only a superficially identifying feature. I donned a dirndl that belonged to my cousin; she'd bought it years ago for a wedding in Salzburg. I'm not even sure which region it's from. Now, for me, it stands for my own history.

I consider the whole traditional-costume thing an indication of how natural Hansi's family must have felt as Austrian Jews. The second district, a dense, narrow strip of land between the Danube River and the Danube Canal, officially called the Leopoldstadt, was once known as the *Mazzesinsel*, or Matzo Island, because so many Jews lived there, in close quarters and for the most part peacefully beside their non-Jewish neighbors. During the Jewish high holidays, services were held in coffeehouses. In the seventeenth century it became the city's Jewish ghetto, which lasted relatively briefly until the Jews were once again expelled from the city. The area lay outside the municipal walls and was swampy and constantly threatened with floods until the Danube River was regulated in the mid-nineteenth century. When the city constitution granted Jews almost complete legal equality in 1867, Vienna became a center of Jewish life, attracting people from all over the Habsburg Empire. Refugees from Galicia and Bukovina came during World War I. In the year my great-grandparents married, over 200,000 Jews lived in the city. About one in ten Viennese were Jewish. And when I moved to New York in 2012, about ten percent of its population was also Jewish.

After Hitler seized power in Germany in 1933, many German Jews fled to neighboring Austria. And many Jews sympathized with the one-party Christian state that Austria officially became in 1934. Compared to the Nazis, it seemed to be the lesser evil. Austrian Jews also enjoyed a relative degree of religious freedom and civil rights. But the new system also made religious education compulsory. That's the only reason, Hansi writes, that he learned which of his classmates in the elementary school on Kleine Sperlgasse were also Jews, because he saw who went to synagogue with him every week and endured the torment of Hebrew lessons and instruction on subjects that were foreign to him. Aside from his grandfather, who didn't eat pork and was on the board of a synagogue, Judaism only appeared a few times a year in family life, just as it had in my childhood. Like many assimilated families, they celebrated the most important holidays of two religions: the Jewish New Year and Yom Kippur, the Day of Atonement, each autumn; Christmas and Hanukkah each winter; Easter and Passover each spring.

In the fall of 1935 Hansi moved from that school to a secondary school on Radetzkystrasse, in the third district. Hansi's cousin had already studied there, and his younger sister was to enroll there the following year.

Maybe his parents hoped things would go better there, and Hansi would finally get good grades so he could go on to other studies. But no. Just a few weeks after starting school, Hansi faked an injury and managed to persuade a doctor at the hospital that his uninjured right hand needed to be put in a cast, so he was freed from homework. No wonder he was soon advised to choose a less academically demanding school. A teacher showed me the archival file of his school record, where a tidy script had noted "Withdrew May 6, 1936." Hansi switched to a four-year, less academically stringent secondary school—a disappointment for the family. The yellowed paper doesn't say why he left so close to the end of the school year. Hansi's papers reveal nothing of it, and no family members can help me. Was it really just his grades—his mid-year report card included not a single

A, and he got a D in natural history, mathematics, and languages—or was there another reason? I'd like to know more, because the three-quarters of a year he spent at the school on Radetzkystrasse was supposed to have significantly shaped his life. But this isn't the first time I find no one's left to tell me about the past.

CHILDHOOD IN VIENNA: HELGA

For my grandmother Helga, remembering has become a sport—a race against oblivion, in which every detail that comes to mind puts her in the lead. Listening to her rewards you with detailed reports, like the fact that, in the years before she began school, she would sneak into her parents' bedroom each morning and crawl into bed with her mother. Her father was already at work. The maid served them breakfast in bed, after having gone to the dairy to refill the milk can.

Or that she often spent mornings with her mother, Hertha, in Alois Drasche Park, in the fourth district. It was one of Hertha's preferred spots because it was just a few blocks from their apartment in the public housing complex on the Margaretengürtel, and almost let her feel as if she lived in one of the magnificent houses overlooking the green.

Helga also recalls her mother dressing her in white shoes and stockings, which she detested because the stockings were attached to her bodice by a ribbon. Hertha herself was elegant and always well-kept. She set little Helga's light-brown hair into curls and made sure her daughter received the appropriate training for young ladies even before school began: piano and voice lessons, dance, English, gymnastics, swimming. Hertha was the daughter of a Protestant aristocratic father and a baptized Jewish mother, and she had a strict upbringing. Until the age of eighteen, she attended a boarding school specifically for officers' daughters, where all the girls had to remain covered up even when showering, wore brown or gray wool uniforms with white aprons, and spoke only French during meals. She was "always a bit prissy," Helga says—her mother came from a well-respected household and hadn't been raised for a life in which she was mostly on her own and had to make her own decisions.

They were proud bourgeois living in public housing, an acquaintance of mine remarks when I describe my grandmother's childhood. There is no such thing anymore. Their most prized possession lay in the dining room: a Persian rug, near the piano which they were still paying off in installments. Two of the apartment's rooms doubled as an office for Hertha's father, a pulmonologist. The waiting room was often so overcrowded on the afternoons he saw patients that the line wound into the staircase. Word had gotten out that he offered free treatment for those who couldn't afford it.

My great-grandfather Paul had attended German language secondary school in Brno and went on to study medicine in Vienna. He worked mornings as a police doctor at two different Viennese inspectorates. The police liked him—especially lower-ranking police, because he always showed sympathy for underdogs.

Her father was a curiously Austrian blend, says Helga: a socialist loyal to the emperor who was also patriotic and interpreted his Judaism liberally. During World War I he had fought for the Habsburg army in Italy and was awarded the Golden Cross of Merit. A wartime lung injury had left him with a slightly curved spine. He regularly sent money to his mother and three siblings back in Moravia. In his Viennese neighborhood, the less distinguished part of the fifth district, he was widely known and well liked.

My great-grandmother Hertha, born in 1905, was baptized at birth, just as her Jewish mother had been. Her father, an officer in the Imperial-Royal Army, came from a respected, albeit impoverished, noble family. As a young officer he had taken a hot air balloon ride, and during a practice maneuver, the balloon caught fire and crashed. He fractured his femur, which subsequently grew infected, and his right leg had to be amputated. Although he was now considered a war hero and received a desk post, the incident put a sudden and unexpected end to his ambitious plans and rankled him for the rest of his life. He became depressed and distant. In 1918, when Hertha was thirteen, her parents divorced. Her mother worked as a nurse; her father soon remarried and spent most of his time at his summer house on an island in part of present-day Croatia, which back then was Italy. He paid his daughter little heed. When Hertha wasn't at boarding school, she lived with her mother.

When Hertha was eighteen, her mother fell ill with uterine cancer. Only now did Hertha—who used to sing scornful songs along with all the other children, *Jud, Jud, spuck in Hut, sag der Mama, das tut gut!* ("Jew, Jew, spit in your hat, tell your Mama it's good, that's that.")—learn of her own Jewish background. By then she had finished school and found work as a secretary at a local cleaning services company, a job she didn't like. While at her mother's bedside in Archduke Rainer Hospital, she met a Jewish assistant doctor. Paul Pollak was thirteen years her elder, promised to take care of her, and said he'd like to start a family. With him, she would never be alone again. They married in 1925, just a few months after Hertha's mother died.

My grandmother Helga was born on February 14, 1929; the previous year, her parents' first child had died shortly after birth, of a heart defect. As a result, Helga was all the more spoiled. Although money was always tight, she was given only the best—private lessons, beautiful clothes, lots of attention. It deeply shaped her character. I believe she developed a self-confidence in those formative years that later made her seem unshakable. As far as I can recall, I never saw her doubt herself. Criticism bounces right off her, which sometimes drives us grandchildren mad. We often asked her to knock before entering our room. To no avail.

Throughout Helga's childhood, poverty loomed on the horizon. Their maid, Minna, for example, lived in a tiny, cordoned-off corner of the kitchen, unimaginable by today's standards. My grandmother remains convinced that such an arrangement was not only common back then, but that Minna was extremely grateful to have work, receive regular payment, and even accommodation. The consequences of the Great Depression ultimately grew noticeable. When

Helga and her parents, Hertha and Paul Pollak, circa 1933.

Helga began elementary school in 1935, about one-fifth of Vienna's entire population was still unemployed.

In 1931 Hertha—who, according to Jewish law, was considered Jewish because her mother was—officially decided to join the Jewish community. So that her child would know where she belonged, she later explained. Each Christmas they still had a Christmas tree and presents, and each Hanukkah they lit the menorah.

At elementary school Helga caught chickenpox. Every day her mother treated her itchy blisters with a white tincture. Helga had noticed for some time that Hertha, whose figure had always been full, now had a huge belly. After taking care of Helga's skin one morning, Hertha explained that she had to go pick up the baby the stork was bringing them. Six-year-old Helga disapproved: "I said, 'Just leave it there, I'm so sick!' She said, 'Well then, we won't get one at all, we'll lose our chance.' I said, 'Then take the next one.'" Helga lost the argument. On April 16, 1936, she got a little sister, Liese.

THE YEAR 1938

A few clicks, and the voice of Kurt von Schuschnigg streams from my computer. He takes long pauses between sentences. "So I now take leave of the Austrian people with a German word of farewell, uttered from the depths of my heart: God protect Austria!" As Helga's father, Paul, listened to the radio broadcast of the federal chancellor's speech on Friday, March 11, 1938, shortly before eight o'clock in the evening, he cried.

For four years, the Austrofascist government strove to keep Hitler at bay. He had repeatedly threatened to invade with his troops, most recently just a few days prior, when Schuschnigg had announced a referendum regarding Austria's independence. On March 11, Schuschnigg resigned and ordered the military to pose no resistance to Nazi Germany.

Helga sat next to her father in the living room—she remembers it to this day. Her mother was visiting relatives in Brno and had taken nearly two-year-old Liese along. So nine-year-old Helga was alone with her despairing father. She cried with him, even though she didn't understand what he was afraid of.

The next day, German troops crossed the Austrian border. On March 13, the new federal chancellor, appointed by the Nazis, officially signed the annexation into law. The following day, Hitler came to Vienna. Jubilant crowds thronged

Mariahilferstrasse, complete with garlands, tanks, and march music. On the morning of March 15, the chancellor of the Reich made an appearance on the balcony of the Hofburg palace. Amid the crowd stood my grandfather Hansi. The twelve-year-old had climbed up a lamppost to get a better look—the sun shone brightly, people beamed, and along with everyone else he shouted *"Sieg Heil!"*

His parents had been horrified as he headed out toward the Heldenplatz, the vast public space facing the palace. All the other Jewish families hid their children at home, but the enthusiasm on the streets fascinated Hansi and he was, as usual, undeterred. I think he probably saw it as just another adventure, one like any other, and its appeal would be diminished only by the depressed mood at home. He had the vague feeling his presence wasn't entirely welcome at the celebration, he writes. But his curiosity outweighed his fear: "As long as you shouted along loud enough, you wouldn't really stand out."

I wonder how Hansi's parents, uncles, and aunts envisioned their future. Did they hope they'd somehow get by and come to terms with the newly uncertain times? That they could avoid attracting attention by shouting along loud enough, or working quietly enough? It's possible that, as the first violent clashes broke out after the *Anschluss*, they weren't yet aware of the imminent threat. Pogroms come and go, many Viennese Jews believed. Scrubbing the ground won't kill you. Hansi's Aunt Sophie was handed a small brush and forced to clean the sidewalk of slogans graffitied by Schuschnigg's supporters in an alley in the third district, surrounded by sneering onlookers. I know this because her daughter, Hansi's cousin Ilse, told me many years later when I visited her in London. Near her parents' furniture store on Seidlgasse there was a taxi stand, she told me in her old-fashioned German, often sprinkled with English words. Her father got along well with the taxi drivers, he knew them all by name and frequently chatted with them. After the Anschluss, they stopped returning his greetings. One month later, when Ilse was eleven years old, her father took his own life.

Initially, my grandmother Helga's life continued as before. Each morning her father brought her to school, the public elementary school on Gassergasse, in the fifth district, two blocks from their apartment. At noon she was picked up by him or the maid. Lunch, nap, homework, piano practice, then off to the park.

In mid-April 1938, before the day's lessons had begun, the school principal entered her third-grade classroom. All the students stood up. Helga and another Jewish girl were called forward. The two would have to leave the school immediately, announced the principal, whose lapel now bore a Nazi party pin. Jews are no longer welcome here. Helga started to cry. As soon as the principal had left the room, the teacher tried to console the girl—she disapproved of her students' exclusion, but was powerless against it: their new school, which was only for Jewish children, would be nice too.

And indeed, it wasn't so bad, even if Helga now had to walk clear across the fifth district each day to the elementary school in the Hundsturm neighborhood, where classes were overcrowded. She liked learning, and the Jewish teachers did their best to teach well and keep order, which wasn't easy because children were constantly leaving. Between 1938 and 1939 about 100,000 Austrian Jews fled the country. The Anschluss had brought with it a flood of new laws, decrees, prohibitions, and orders regulating the Jewish population. Jewish officials in government were dismissed; journalists, lawyers, actors, and musicians were banned from work; and schoolchildren, older students, and teachers were expelled from schools and universities. The Nuremberg race laws stipulated who was Jewish and who was not, and systematic expropriations were regular occurrences. It all happened so fast that the persecuted had no chance to analyze the situation. And new restrictions were constantly being added.

This move from one school to the other remains etched in Helga's memory as a humiliating, traumatic turning point. She felt defenseless, she later says. For the first time, people were making it clear that she didn't belong. Rarely have I heard her state, in no uncertain terms, how such injustices hurt her. She simply isn't sentimental, she usually says, emphasizing how she got used to such situations, or that there were people who made it slightly more bearable. And that's still how she sees it: it's important that the teacher consoled her, I mustn't forget to write that down too.

"PREFERABLY ALL TOGETHER..."

The heading "Family members" appears above a box on page two of the form. This box is divided into ten lines. Eight of them have been filled in by Hansi's Aunt Frieda: she lists herself and her fifteen-year-old daughter, Litzi; her older sister, Sophie, and Sophie's eleven-year-old daughter, Ilse; her twin sister, Rosa, who was Hansi's mother; and Rosa's family—namely, Hansi, his father Moritz, and his brother Herbert. Below that is a pre-printed question: "Which of the aforementioned family members are to emigrate now, and which later?" Her immediate family first, wrote Frieda, "but preferably all together."

This form had been issued in early May 1938 by the Emigration Department of the Welfare Center of the Jewish Community of Vienna. The Austrian Jewish Community, which had represented the interests of local Jews since 1852 and served as an umbrella organization of 440 Jewish associations in Vienna alone, had for the most part been closed within days of the Anschluss. But just two months later they opened again, newly restructured: in addition to promulgating the new Nazi laws, their other main task was referred to as "emigration." The community had pledged to the Nazi regime that it would persuade 20,000 destitute Jews to "emigrate" the following year. Such people weren't hard to find.

The community distributed two-page "emigration forms" that collected data including their name, occupation, income, and family members, as well as their preferred destination and any relationships with people abroad. Within the first three weeks, 40,000 people came forward. Including Frieda.

It's unusual to have written the names of eight relatives on the "emigration form," the Jewish community archivist explains as she zooms in on the scanned gray sheet on her screen. Such a high number is rare. I'm a bit proud of my great-great-aunt Frieda, whom I never met. The many names on the form must mean she was more devoted to her family than most. Right?

My great-grandfather Moritz also filled out the same form; his is dated May 10, 1938. His couldn't look more different than his sister-in-law's. The scans show how Frieda's form had passed through many hands—it's full of seals, stamps, and annotations, and its edges appear worn. And no fewer than seventeen additional pages are attached. Moritz's form, on the other hand, is empty except for his own information. Its paper looks smooth, and not a single other page is attached.

Moritz's handwriting, which I'm seeing here for the first time, is loopy and confident. When asked for "previous occupation and most recent position," he simply replied "businessman." To the question "Have you learned a new trade? If so, what?" he replied "house painter." That's odd, I think. In a situation like that, wouldn't you have been expected to outline your skills in detail? Even in listing relatives he seems to have been less solicitous than his sister-in-law, filling in only four people: his wife, his two sons, and a sixteen-year-old niece.

Moritz probably filled out the form less carefully because he guessed his chances of emigrating were low. He declared having nothing to fund his own emigration, which would be a problem since the Nazi regime did its utmost to seize Jews' assets before they left the country. "Emigration taxes," "atonement fees," and payments to the national "Emigration Fund" were due, so you had to provide pricey evidence you'd obtained the necessary permits and paid for steamer tickets, foreign currency exchange, and visas on your own.

In order to qualify for an entry visa to the United States, you also had to have an American citizen willing to file an affidavit guaranteeing they would take care of the refugees. The third major hurdle was a restrictive immigration law that set a quota based on how many people from a particular country were already living in the United States. There were too few places for the refugees trying to flee the territory now under Nazi control: by June 1939, 309,000 German, Austrian, and Czech Jews had applied for 27,000 available spots.

My great-grandfather, it seems, had been more realistic than his sister-in-law—a point often reiterated in Hansi's notes. His father, he writes, accurately assessed situations, possibilities, and risks, and made wise decisions in accordance with the circumstances. Later on, that's what saved his son's life.

The seventeen scanned pages attached to my great-great-aunt Frieda's form allow me to understand what happened to the family between May 1938 and November 1939: the first page details the Jewish communal organization's "home check" and describes their living situation in keywords. Shortly after the Anschluss, Frieda's husband had been arrested because one of his vendors had filed a false complaint against him, presumably hoping to take over his furniture business. "Business liquidated—nothing kept," it reads. An administrator appointed by the Nazi regime had taken over the operation and dissolved it within a few months. As a result, Frieda and her fifteen-year-old daughter, Litzi, were left to rely on the Jewish community's welfare program, receiving thirty Reichsmarks a month and meals from the food bank. In August 1938 they could no longer afford their own apartment, or perhaps they were evicted. Frieda moved in with her twin sister, Hansi's mother, where she shared a room with her daughter. Years before, prior to the birth of Rosa's sons, the sisters and their husbands had lived together for a while.

"Affidavit obtained from cousin," wrote the Jewish community representative who checked on their living situation. How had my great-great-aunt Frieda managed that? She knew that her now imprisoned husband had a cousin named Israel Simochowski, who had emigrated to New York shortly after the turn of the century and Americanized his name, going by Irving Simon. No one had had any contact with him since.

I send Frieda's granddaughter, a psychologist living in the New York suburbs, an email asking how Frieda found her

Ilse, Hansi, Litzi, and Fritz circa 1930.

cousin: she'd gotten hold of a New York phone book and looked for her husband's cousin's name. "I'd guess she found a lot of entries with that name and wrote them all. Fortunately, one of them was him." Irving agreed to issue the affidavit. Frieda's next step was to apply for a visa at the American embassy. Compared to many Austrian Jews, her odds for getting a spot under the quota system were better: her husband had been born in Kiev and his Russian citizenship applied to his family by extension; fewer people were applying under the Russian quota than the Austrian one.

Meanwhile, Frieda and her sisters looked for ways to get

their children out of the country. Frieda's husband was in prison, and in April 1938 Sophie's husband had taken his own life. Hansi's parents were the only ones still together. In the wake of the November pogroms, as representatives of the Jewish community in Britain began organizing transportation and accommodation for persecuted children, they signed up all of the family's five children: Hansi and his brother, Herbert; Sophie's children, Ilse and Fritz; and Frieda's daughter, Litzi. There were more applications than available seats, which is why orphans and those whose parents were in custody were given preference. So Litzi, Ilse, and Fritz got a spot, but Hansi and Herbert didn't. In December 1938, they said their goodbyes at the train station. The others would soon follow, they said.

Even though they had grown up together like siblings, Hansi only mentions his cousins' escape in passing. Is this a question of indifference, repression, or simple forgetting? All these years later, it's Ilse, who stayed in London and became an elementary school teacher, and Litzi, who moved to New York, who tell me what it was like to leave Vienna and their family. Ilse had to cut off her long, black braids before departure. Braiding her hair was enough of a production that the twelve-year-old couldn't do it on her own, and who knew whether she'd find anyone who'd lend a hand in England. I compare the last picture taken before her departure with one taken a few months earlier. She looks years older with the pageboy haircut, I think. Her hand rests on her mother's shoulder, their heads almost touching.

Litzi, then sixteen, was looking forward to the journey. She's a little ashamed of that now, she tells me during my visit to her home on Long Island. She was one of the few who had learned English at school and couldn't wait to put it to use. As she bade her parents goodbye at the station, her father, recently released from prison, cried. Her mother maintained her composure. "We'll see each other again," she told her daughter. And Litzi believed her.

In August or September 1939, Litzi's parents finally got an entry visa for the United States. It was valid only for two people. The rest of the pages attached to Frieda's form document the bureaucratic gauntlet that now lay before them. They'd have to go through innumerable official channels set up by the Nazi regime for maximum laboriousness, and designed to exact the greatest expense. Anyone wanting to take valuables with them had to pay a 100% surcharge. Securities and insurance couldn't be executed. Obtaining a tax return—just one of several pieces of proof required to leave the country—meant collecting documents from four different authorities. Then came the "political safety clearance," "certificate of good conduct" to prove you had no police record, and proof that housing had been secured; you needed a new passport, had to provide a list of all your assets, and then, when you finally had an exit visa in hand, you were given a mere fourteen days to leave the country. Otherwise, you could be deported to a concentration camp. Outside countless offices and embassies, the SS whipped people as they waited in line.

The bureaucracy was vexatious. The family only received a tax-clearance declaration "as a favor," I read in a letter Litzi's father wrote to the "esteemed Jewish communal organization," also attached to Frieda's form. I wonder if "as a favor" meant in return for a bribe, which was apparently quite common. The tax clearance was only valid for three months. After all that, he found himself without money to pay for their travel, and the steamer tickets would cost 865 Reichsmarks. He had already sent two telegrams to relatives in the United States. But he also knew the local religious community received financial support from British and American Jewish organizations. "Therefore, I see no other option than to turn to my esteemed religious community, and I implore you to help us obtain two steamer tickets," he writes. "It would really be terribly sad if, with all the necessities already lined up, we were to lose the chance of a lifetime solely because we couldn't get steamer tickets."

On November 7, 1939, he received an appointment with the "Emigration Department—Customs Clearance Group" of the Jewish communal organization, I learn from another pre-printed sheet attached to Frieda's form. The next page is full of handwritten notes and several stamped seals, all dated early November 1939. "2 steamer tickets 865 Reichsmarks ($346)." "Tickets paid for in Amsterdam," someone noted on November 12, 1939. At the last minute, the money from the United States had come through. Their American cousin, Irving Simon, a butcher by trade, had sold his car for it.

Litzi still has her parents' tickets. On November 22, 1939, Frieda and her husband boarded a Holland America Line steamer in Rotterdam: 3rd Class, Cabin 553, Bed D, and Cabin 592, Bed B. Its destination was Hoboken, New Jersey.

Twin sisters Frieda and Rosa had spent their entire lives together. They looked alike—same dark, chin-length curls, same slightly starry-eyed gaze, same stocky figure—and had always found it funny when others confused them. They often walked hand in hand on the street. They spent Sundays, vacations, and holidays together. And for the last few months, they had once again shared the same apartment. All that was now over. Frieda left, and Sophie and Rosa stayed in Vienna.

"Preferably all together . . . " Frieda, full of hope, had naively written on the form just a year and a half earlier. In March 1938, my grandfather's family had consisted of six adults and five children. As I gather information on their various fates, I wonder what the sisters thought and said when they parted. Did they realize the family had been destroyed? Maybe they didn't view the situation so hopelessly. Everyone had left promising to look for any and every opportunity to bring the rest of the family along later on. When Ilse spent some time at a Quaker boarding school in southern England, she repeatedly asked if they had room for her two cousins, but the school was already overcrowded. She learned English, although her Austrian accent remained strong, since she was there with so many fellow refugee kids. When war broke out in September 1939, escape to England became impossible. Ilse's brother, Fritz, went to Sydney, where a Jewish family took him in. They tried to obtain a visa for his mother, but the complex process slowly dragged on. Frieda and her husband went to New York, where they started out living with Irving and his wife as they looked for work. Later, once they could afford their own apartment, they opened a small furniture store in the Bronx and scraped together enough money to bring over their daughter, who had been placed with a host family in Liverpool. Then they tried to get their other relatives out of Vienna. Maybe they would all be together again soon.

"EMIGRATE? YOU'VE GOT TO BE KIDDING!"

Pleased at having found the "emigration forms" Hansi's family filled out, I ask the staff of the Jewish community archives in Vienna whether they have those of Helga's family. They check, but don't find any. I decide to ask Helga the next time I see her. The weekly dinner hosted by my aunt is a good opportunity: every Monday the family gathers there, and now that I'm back in Vienna I do my best not to miss it. Grandma Helga doesn't eat much for dinner, but she likes to come down from her apartment on the second floor to join us.

I ask whether she knew if her father completed an "emigration form" in the early summer of 1938. She looks at me. "You've got to be kidding!" she replies, sounding indignant and sad at the same time. In the first few months after the Anschluss, no one in her family had even mentioned the idea of emigrating.

Shortly after the Anschluss, her father, Paul, had been suspended from his job as a doctor in the police department and then forced to retire, even though he was only forty-six. Almost everywhere else, Jews were simply fired. Retirement was therefore a special concession his superiors had made, allowing him to receive a pension. It didn't seem all that bad, says Helga. Her father was convinced he'd be able to find another job under the new regime. That's just how he was,

Helga adds, always looking on the bright side. Now that he was down and out, he expected or hoped others would offer him the same solidarity he'd always shown those weaker than himself.

A little later his family, just like two thousand other Jewish tenants in Vienna's public housing, received an eviction notice. Vienna's social democratic city government had built 66,000 public housing units since the end of World War I—a lot, but not enough to contain the booming population. When the German Reich began moving political and military personnel to Vienna, living quarters grew even scarcer. The eviction of "non-Aryans" was officially sanctioned. They were to clear the premises by July 1, 1938.

A scan of the eviction notice is preserved in the Archives of the Austrian Resistance. I look at the form, filled out by hand. The illegible scrawl next to the preprinted "reason for eviction" probably reads "Jew" or "non-Aryan." Several documents are attached to the main form, which is how I discover that my great-grandfather filed an objection within a week of receiving the notice. On May 30, 1938, he fed a sheet into his typewriter and replied: "Since I will only be able to secure another apartment in August and, as a war veteran injured on the front lines—I am a doctor for the police department (currently on leave)—I have not yet been informed of the exact details concerning the pension to which I am entitled, and hence cannot yet know what living arrangements I will be able to afford, I ask that I be granted an extension to stay in public housing until the month of August. I vow to vacate the apartment by the August deadline." The city housing authority's response came twelve days later and is also archived: No extensions permitted.

Might my great-grandfather have started to harbor some doubts by then? I wonder whether he and his wife might have had some disagreements. Was my great-grandmother Hertha as feisty back then as she later became, once she was on her own? Hurry up, fill out the "emigration form" and look for relatives or acquaintances who can send an affidavit or otherwise help get you out of the country, I want to implore them through the years. I know how this will end.

But no. On June 30, 1938, Paul had to fill out a four-page form, "Jewish Property Inventory." He had 100 Reichsmarks in a passbook, his gold pocket watch and the silverware were worth 200 Reichsmarks, and he possessed 200 Reichsmarks worth of medical instruments and books. He estimated the value of his life insurance policy at 1,200 Reichsmarks. He didn't yet know how much his pension would be worth. If the information he gave is correct, the family had virtually no savings, and certainly not enough to cover the costly emigration of four people. So maybe Paul didn't even try because he was well aware they stood no chance. All around him, tens of thousands of Jews were desperately trying to leave the country. Surely he'd heard how expensive, difficult, and therefore often hopeless it was.

Couldn't you find someone, anyone to borrow money from? I want to beg him. "Papa had a bit of a blind spot," says Helga. As always, when it comes to her father, she speaks with a little more hesitation than usual. She doesn't want to judge him for his decisions. At the time, they seemed reasonable.

The family moved into a new apartment in mid-June 1938, on Margaretenstrasse in the fifth district, and it was nicer and bigger than the one they'd had in public housing, Helga recalls. Even though a Jewish doctor and his wife were already living there—and they were trying to emigrate to the United States—there was still enough space; the building even had several balconies and an exercise room. And it was the first time Helga lived in an apartment with a private bathroom. Before that, she had always had to take sponge baths in her bedroom, with water warmed on the stove and poured into a little tub.

It also boasted a basic doctor's office, and Paul continued to receive patients. Like all Jewish physicians, his license and national health insurance certification had been revoked, but as a "Jewish healthcare provider" he was one of the few still permitted to treat Jewish patients. Because Jews were now only allowed to see Aryan doctors if their lives were in imminent danger, patients came to his practice from far and wide. Before the Anschluss, he had charged many patients little or nothing if they couldn't afford it. Now Jews from all walks of life were coming to him. Business was good, and Paul was earning more than before. His confidence in Austria had been restored, and the inconveniences of the regime change seemed to have blown over.

The first time Helga tells me her family's situation improved after the Anschluss, I'm sure I've misunderstood her. Since I've begun looking into my family history, I've been reading about many people's differing destinies. But never have I heard a sentence like that. So I'm compelled to ask: "After the Anschluss things got better for the family?" Absolutely—financially things were going well, and that was important because her father still had to support his mother and siblings in Brno. So not only did the idea of emigrating strike her father as dishonorable—after all, he was a decorated World War I veteran—it would have been irresponsible. Their rights were limited under the new regime, but they'd just have to learn to make do.

*

"It was October 19, 1938," says Helga. When she came home from school that day, a Wednesday, her father was gone. In the photos the secret state police—the Gestapo—took after his arrest, he wears a jacket with a pocket handkerchief, a white shirt, and a patterned necktie. His side-parted hair is precisely cut and neatly combed. He looks as if he's headed to an important meeting. Did he think it was all a misunderstanding and that he would soon be released?

The Gestapo locked him up in solitary at the police detention center of the Rossauer Barracks, a massive reddish-brown building on the banks of the Danube Canal. Compared to the many Gestapo detainees who were tortured and didn't survive detention, things went rather well for Paul. Clearly his former police department coworkers campaigned for him, because he'd been popular; although he was now imprisoned, he was allowed to write to his wife every Sunday. He was given ruled paper, which he folded once, so that his letters were about the size of a postcard. Using a pencil, he filled the narrow lines with a steady cursive I can barely read. "Stapo detainee cell 26," he scribbled along the edge. Helga saved all her parents' correspondence.

"I had imagined celebrating our wedding anniversary rather differently," Paul writes four days after his arrest, on October 23, 1938. "You cannot imagine what receiving your note meant to me in my desolate solitude, so I beg of you, write me often, because the thought of you is the only thing that can give me some will to live." My great-grandmother Hertha obliged, writing several letters and postcards every week. She delivered many of them in person, because she was allowed to take her husband's clothes home to wash. "I'm always happy when I've got your dirty laundry in hand, although I'm also glad there's not too much of it," she writes. She wasn't allowed to actually see or speak to Paul.

He wrote telling her not to inform his family in Brno about his arrest. He didn't want to upset them, so he told her to say he had a broken arm and couldn't write. "As far as Franziska Alice is concerned," he goes on, "she should cling to Uncle Gustav, so as not to suddenly find herself in Aunt Valerie's situation; Gustav, with his rich and influential relatives, could do a lot." He'd now begun writing his letters in a code of sorts, encrypting names. Franziska Alice is none other than Hertha herself. Aunt Valerie's husband, a Christian Socialist, was deported to Dachau. Who Uncle Gustav might have been, Helga no longer knows. "I'm sure Franziska's fate won't be the same as Valerie's," my great-grandmother replied a few days later.

"Since, luckily, there's nobody around to laugh at me, I read all your notes countless times, day and night," Paul confesses on November 5. "Just imagine, I have to think, now Helga's going to school, now our two curly heads are in their little beds, and who knows when I'll get to see all that again?" Who could know? Back home Hertha, now suddenly solely responsible for her family, used her meticulous hand-writing to send letter after letter to her husband's friends, acquaintances, and former colleagues, asking them to stand up for Paul. Writing in code, she tells him about it: "You need to know, this much is certain: regarding the condition of Chayela's eldest boy, you needn't worry too much. The child is strong. Of course, it will take some time for him to fully recuperate."

From his letters, I can sense that Paul finally realized how dangerous the regime was for him too. He didn't know why the Gestapo arrested him, nor did he know if or when he would be released. He writes Hertha that she should contact a friend in Zurich and ask him to look into emigration options there. Paul was desperate, insecure, and lonely. "Please don't leave me, and write to me often," he begs. "I assure you: the lines of your letters are the axis upon which my whole life revolves, from which I gain strength and renewed courage, though I find it very difficult." The words "very difficult" are written in all caps and underlined.

I'm moved by these letters. Although my great-grandfather now realized he'd have to leave the country, he still had no idea what other people would prove capable of. He complained of insomnia, nervousness, and boredom. The letters often mention laundry. Did he know how good he had it compared to other Gestapo prisoners? At least you have enough to eat, I want to tell my great-grandfather, and nobody's beating you. Of course I'm being unfair; I have the advantage of twenty-twenty hindsight. And no matter how bearable the conditions might have been, Paul was still wrongfully imprisoned, with no prospect of being put on trial or released.

He was probably also cut off from news of current events. It isn't clear from my great-grandparents' correspondence whether Paul had heard about the pogroms that took place the night of November 9, 1938, for example. I'm unable to understand the hints my great-grandmother Hertha included in her letters until her daughter Helga points them out to me: "We haven't seen much of our friends in the last few days, everyone's staying home as much as possible. I haven't sent Helga to school since Wednesday, she's so happy to stay home," Hertha wrote two days after Kristallnacht, which took place on a Wednesday. She promised Helga would diligently continue practicing piano. Paul didn't write to ask why his eldest daughter, who had always loved going to school, had suddenly changed her mind. Might he have suspected Helga was staying home for fear of further uprisings? It wasn't until the following weekend, on November 20, that Paul remarked how he missed Hertha's "usual optimism." In her reply, she assured him it had nothing to do with her situation: "The general bad mood among our friends and relatives got the upper hand over me too."

"Beloved, dearest wife! I'm leaving tomorrow, I'm feeling hardy and brave, as should you—be strong. Farewell, and give everyone a kiss for me, your faithful Paul." He underlined the words "I'm feeling hardy and brave." The postcard reached my great-grandmother on December 3, 1938. What they had long feared had now happened: Paul had been sent to a concentration camp. The Nazis had been deporting German and Austrian Jews to Buchenwald—the camp near the German city of Weimar—for some time already, forcing them to emigrate. Those who had entry visas from another country, plus the approval of the Reich's Main Security Office and the Gestapo, were allowed out again.

Again, Hertha sat down and wrote to anyone and everyone who might be able to help. A letter an acquaintance wrote on her behalf got all the way to Prussian Field Marshal August von Mackensen, another went directly to the Gestapo in Berlin; she enclosed thank-you letters written by "prominent Aryans" expressing praise for Paul, as well as a character witness statement from their maid, Minna, who they'd since had to dismiss. My grandmother also saved her mother's correspondence with various consulates in Vienna: Hertha had spoken to the British and American embassies without success, but the Chinese embassy finally confirmed that the family would be permitted to enter Shanghai. Which meant that Paul would soon be released.

Hertha closed out Paul's savings account and life insurance, and bought a steamer ticket for her husband. She and their daughters would follow later on—they weren't in immediate danger, and they kept hearing how Jewish detainees were particularly harassed at Buchenwald. But then, with no explanation, Paul wasn't released. Hertha returned the ticket and paid the cancellation fee. Because the market of furnishings that desperate Jews were trying to sell was saturated, she sold their Persian rug far below its value and bought a new ticket. Paul's release was delayed once more, and the family never learned why. Once again Hertha returned the ticket, replacing the diamond on her wedding ring with a less expensive stone. The proceeds were just enough for one ticket. Hertha then returned the piano Helga had been practicing on, as she could no longer pay the installments.

When I ask Helga what her experience of this particular period was like—her father's imprisonment, her mother's attempts to arrange for their emigration—she mentions how depressed the mood was at home, her mother's fear, their slide toward poverty. They often ran out of money well before the end of the month. Hertha then went to the Dorotheum, the pawnshop, and pawned the few silver objects she had left. The small loan helped her get by until her husband's pension, which the family relied on, arrived a few days later—and then she'd reclaim the silver again.

On June 10, 1939, Paul was released. He was allowed to stay in Vienna for two days before moving on to Genoa, from where his ship would depart. He hadn't seen ten-year-old Helga for nine months. And he had changed. His face was emaciated, his front teeth had been knocked out in Buchenwald, and his scalp was shaved. He was trembling, nervous, and anxious. When a gust of wind blew the hat off his head on the way to the station, he ran after it crying.

Helga doesn't dwell on such episodes. She prefers to talk about the people who helped her during this time—her maternal grandfather in particular, who resumed a major role in her life. Hertha's father, a retired officer of the Austro-Hungarian Imperial Army, spent most of the year at his home in Lussinpiccolo, now known as Mali Lošinj, on the Croatian island of Lošinj. Once, when she was five or six, Helga had visited with her mother, and she remembers a terrarium in her grandfather's garden with a reptile she describes as a little alligator. A few months after the Anschluss, the lieutenant colonel abandoned his summer house and returned to Vienna with his second wife, Gabriela, whom everyone called Ella. Did they move so he could support his daughter, who was now on her own? Or because it was too expensive to run two households? Or for political reasons? "I don't know," says Helga. Her grandfather spoke with his former comrades, some of whom were now in the upper echelons of the Nazi party, and helped support the family with a little money and food.

There were also others who stood by them: Ella's brother, a stormtrooper, spoke up for them; their former maid, Minna, who continued to visit, and her husband, also a Nazi party member, remained loyal to the family; a former colleague of Helga's father; a Czech relative; the list goes on. They're all important, Helga says. "He's definitely part of the story," I often hear her say. I nod but can barely keep track. I'm not writing a phone book, I say to myself, and immediately feel disrespectful. Of course these people were important. They made Helga feel her world was still halfway decent.

In mid-June 1939 Helga's family got some news from Genoa. Paul discovered they'd been cheated; the steamer she'd bought him a ticket on didn't exist. He'd gone there with a six-month tourist visa, and foreign Jews in Italy weren't granted a longer residence permit. Nor could the Italian authorities deport him to the German Reich, because he wouldn't have been admitted. He was stuck.

"ARYANS ONLY"

Until 1938, the furniture shop on Margaretenstrasse had supported Hansi's family. Its storefront and small workshop were permeated by the scent of glue and varnish. A horse-drawn delivery wagon was usually parked out front. Moritz, Hansi's father, ran the business. He enjoyed the work, although business hadn't exactly boomed following the Great Depression. Every sale posed a risk because most customers set up payment plans, and installments often had to be chased down. By the time Germany annexed Austria, the family had nearly exhausted its savings, and was obliged to dismiss the nanny and cook they had previously been able to afford.

On April 13, 1938, a law was passed allowing the Nazi-appointed Reich Governor—who was in charge of "coordination," meaning forced political conformity—to appoint so-called acting administrators for Jewish enterprises. The administrators' task was to oversee such businesses' expropriation. The man assigned to Moritz's furniture business set about collecting all customers' outstanding payments. It's hard to say whether the largely non-Jewish clientele had been intimidated or impressed by his stormtrooper uniform, but either way, he'd collected all debts within a few months. Because all revenue went to him as a reward for his work, there was no money to fund ongoing production. The business closed that autumn. No compensation was offered. Hansi's report ends laconically: "I can remember my father's relief upon being rid of dealing with that parasitic Nazi party bigwig on a daily basis."

Today not a trace of the furniture shop can be found. The larger building it was a part of no longer exists, and the storefront of the building that took its place, now painted blue, is a pizzeria. How odd that there are no photos, I think—my great-grandfather had always enjoyed taking pictures. The so-called Aryanization files, in which the expropriating administrator documented the business's liquidation, are nowhere to be found in the Austrian State Archives. What a shame—I'd have liked to know the acting administrator's name, where he lived, and whether he'd taken notes on how the Jewish proprietor, my great-grandfather, had reacted.

But then a helpful historian, who had given me an overview of what I might look for in which archive, sends me her big discovery: the Aryanization files of another furniture shop, on Seidlgasse in the third district, which had belonged to Hansi's Aunt Sophie and her husband. Scrolling through the scans, I find pages upon pages of lists: outstanding payments, debts to be collected, inventories. The file also includes correspondence between the acting administrator and his superior, the "Private Sector State Commissioner—Acting Administrators' Inspection Office." In April 1938 the acting administrator took over the business, and in December it closed permanently.

These documents are brutally sober. "The owner killed himself the day before the acting administrator was appointed," reads one "activity report." "Since I had determined the business's status was inactive due to tax arrears, foreign currency racketeering, etc., Aryanization was out of the question, so I had to oversee its liquidation." The administrator proudly reports having sold the warehouse cheaply and, moreover, successfully getting the Gestapo to cancel the title transfer papers that had already been issued to a "Jewish usurer" so that the administrator could ultimately obtain the balance of 6,847.14 Reichsmarks. The owner's surviving family—Hansi's Aunt Sophie and her daughter—received 323.33 Reichsmarks, which they then used to cover the funeral and their living expenses.

And suddenly I'm relieved that the files on my great-grandparents' business no longer exist. I find these documents more depressing than the deportation lists, death certificates, and letters I had managed to find. The latter might have made me feel uncomfortably close to death and despair, but they gave little indication of the perpetrator's perspective. The Aryanization files, on the other hand, bring me closer to the culprit—a lot closer. They reveal, in detail, one cog in this massive machinery of annihilation. I see how seriously the administrator took his task. For half a year he carefully prepared lists, scoured warehouses, wrote letters, calculated balance sheets. This is how my family was destroyed, and I can still read all about it today.

After his own furniture business had been expropriated, my great-grandfather Moritz eked out a living as an appraiser, confirming the condition and value of furniture taken from the houses of Jews who had fled or been evicted. He also gradually sold off the family's remaining goods—most likely including his camera, because I cannot find any family photos from after the Anschluss.

The last photo of his two sons is from 1937. Both wear dark shorts and white shirts; Herbert also wears a pale jacket. They are almost the same size, and each has an arm around the other's shoulder. There's a bridge in the background—maybe they're by the Danube Canal. Herbert is around nine years old, and smiles. It looks a little like he's squinting or almost grimacing, perhaps blinded by the sun. Hansi, then about twelve, seems unperturbed. As in almost all other family photos, he doesn't look directly into the camera but tilts his head to the side and peers askance, as if trying to secretly spy on someone or furtively misbehave.

In the photo, I feel like I can see how different the two brothers were: Hansi, the hooligan; Herbert, the intellectual. Hansi liked marching to his own drummer; Herbert easily fell into line. Hansi trespassed in parks, refused to obey teachers, and snuck out of his parents' house whenever he wanted. Herbert was obedient, an avid reader, and liked to draw. Some of his drawings still survive: landscapes, castles, and portraits in pencil and ink, made up of meticulous, minuscule strokes. Certain details—shepherd's crook, cat's paw, gargoyle—look real. But he also had an eye for composition: he knew when to leave a spot blank and when to merely make a visual hint.

Herbert and Hansi, 1937.

Their school report cards also show their differences: Hansi finished the eighth grade in early summer 1939 with an F in four subjects; Herbert's shining seventh-grade report card from May 1942 has a whole row of A's, except for one B in Hebrew.

That report card was from the orphanage for Jewish boys on Grünentorgasse, in the ninth district. By no means were all the children and adolescents there orphans. Herbert, who turned fourteen in January 1942, attended classes because his father, Moritz, was a child-care worker there. After the furniture shop had been shut down, he had taken a continuing education class through the Jewish community and learned to garden. In September 1939, the communal administration hired him as a houseparent at an orphanage for Jewish children on Bauernfeldgasse. Did he actually work there as a gardener? A few months later, in a document from February 1940, he appears as an assistant child-care worker. When the Nazis shut down the orphanage in November 1940, the remaining children moved to the former Jewish apprentices' home on Grünentorgasse.

Hansi held onto his brother's last report card, but none of his own school records. As I examine Herbert's grades, I flash back to the day in February 1996 when I got my own first report card. On the left was a column listing each subject; on the right my teacher had written one word down the entire sheet: "excellent." Of course I had to inform my grandfather, whom I considered the head of our family. By then he spent most of the time in his bedroom: he'd been diagnosed with cancer a month earlier, and the tumor had been removed, but the doctors were powerless over the metastases that had spread throughout his body. In Hansi's last few months, his bedroom became our gathering place. As I remember it, whenever one of us knocked and went in, someone was already there, sitting at the foot of his double bed or on one of the black chairs with pale blue cushions that had gradually wandered over from the dining room.

Hansi studied the report card as if it were some important document and praised me extensively for my straight As. Then he handed me some banknotes. I remember my mother

protesting that he was a "fiend" for resorting to such infla-
tionary rewards. He had pressed 100 German marks into my
palm. Never before had I had that much money. My father
was living in Munich at the time, and my mother and I spent
weekends there. On our next visit, I turned that reward into
a shiny silver Game Boy, complete with the new Super Mario
game, and a BABY born doll, the toy store's hottest item.

I was aware my reward was overly generous, but I had
no way of understanding why Hansi had done it. Back then
I was convinced he would recover from his disease, but he
knew better. The reward was an advance for all the good
grades I had yet to earn. And now, as I hold the report card of
Hansi's little brother in my hands, I recognize another reason
for his generosity: I reminded him of Herbert.

*

Following the anti-Semitic uprisings in the immediate wake
of the Nazis' 1938 arrival in Vienna—after which even the
Völkischer Beobachter, the official party newspaper, exhorted
Austrians to curb their "exuberant radicalism"—Vienna
calmed down over the summer. Then, on November 7,
Herschel Grynszpan assassinated German diplomat Ernst
vom Rath in Paris. The regime saw this as an excuse to take
"revenge" against Jews throughout the Reich. During the night
of November 9–10, in Vienna alone, forty-two synagogues and
prayer houses were destroyed, ninety-six more were devastat-
ingly vandalized, and many Jewish businesses were plundered.

Hansi wrote one and a half pages about that night. He titled the passage "Father," but he starts out narrating an encounter with an acquaintance who was angry that "European Jews were just letting themselves be slaughtered without any resistance." Hansi considered that assessment erroneous: when would anyone have been able to mount a resistance? Hansi clearly felt it was important he explain his father's behavior: "Fundamentally, he wasn't a coward," he writes of Moritz, who had been wounded several times in battle on the front in World War I.

Hansi remembers Moritz as a good father. He always kept his wits about him, writes Hansi, even on that November night: "Kristallnacht—when stormtroopers and mobs roused us from bed in the middle of the night at gunpoint and, right before our eyes, one stormtrooper simply took my father's pocket watch and wedding ring from the nightstand—was certainly no time for heroics. It would have been equally pointless for my mother to have tried to stop the women who'd broken into the apartment from stealing our linens." A man in uniform held a gun to a child's head, writes Hansi, and demanded their jewelry, money, and valuables. The parents obeyed. My grandfather doesn't say whether the child was himself or his brother.

Then the uniformed men led Hansi's father away. "What's going to happen to him?" Hansi's mother asked. "He's going to be shot." Moritz was taken under a so-called emergency arrest. More than 6,500 Jewish people, mostly men, were arrested and severely beaten that night, and the majority of them were later deported to Dachau. Moritz got lucky. The locked basement he was taken to was guarded by a former World War I comrade whom he'd fought alongside at the front. He let Moritz escape. Perhaps his comrade pushed him aside in the crowd or convinced the SS men that Moritz wasn't even a Jew. Hansi's mention of the fact that his father barely escaped arrest is so brief and laconic that I wonder if he even knew what had happened there.

Many survivors describe the November pogrom— *Kristallnacht* or the Night of Broken Glass—as the turning point when they realized how brutal the regime was becoming toward Jews. Even thirteen-year-old Hansi must have been aware of it. At first I'm puzzled by how he seems to feel a need to justify how his father behaved that night: "Only specific situations call for 'heroics,'" Hansi writes, and goes on to tell of Moritz's medals of valor and the Warsaw Ghetto uprising, when a "destined group" of people came together and fought. But on November 9, 1938, his parents' situation didn't meet those prerequisites for heroic deeds, simply because they wanted to protect their sons. Thus, for the first time ever, he witnessed their complete defenselessness.

*

In early summer 1939, Hansi finished his fourth year of secondary school; he had been transferred to a Jewish school for his last year of study. As a Jew, he was forbidden to attend school past the compulsory age. Under normal circumstances, that would have posed some difficulty, but because he'd gotten such bad grades, he wouldn't have been able to move to the next grade anyway. "Nobody really paid any attention to how poorly I'd finished my schooling," he writes. The parents who had previously been so worried about his disobedience had long ago given up on him. "Everybody was glad when we all just got home unscathed each evening." They had other worries. My grandfather was relieved to be done with school: "When you aren't allowed to go to school, you don't have to learn anything anymore, and you don't have to rack your brains or worry about homework," he writes. "These marginalizing measures weren't scary to a student who didn't do well in school—on the contrary, they were a relief, since my future plans were nonexistent." As a Jew, Hansi wasn't allowed to study anyway. The fact that he was looking for a job made sense, since his father's salary didn't even cover basic meals. On top of that, school had become dangerous. The Hitler Youth often started fights each afternoon, beating Jewish students with rubber truncheons. Hansi had always zealously defended himself.

So Hansi contacted the employment office. Since there was a shortage of labor throughout the German Reich, he quickly got a job at a road construction company; as a Jew, according to law, he could only be hired at the lowest pay grade. He soon proved unfit for the job: "Back then, there were no ball bearing, rubber-tired wheelbarrows, only wooden carts with ironclad, wooden wheels, which you had to pull. They were so heavy I could hardly move one when it was loaded with cobblestones. Pulling those carts through soft, often muddy ground was exhausting for strong, full-grown men, and nearly impossible for boys of fourteen or fifteen. The company clearly realized that, and promptly fired me."

Shortly thereafter he was hired by an agricultural machinery manufacturer in the twenty-first district who, of his own initiative, provided his Jewish workers with a yellow armband. "Interacting with his Christian workers was unpredictable. I remember being whacked on the head by a fellow worker once, for no reason, to the point that my eardrum must have been blown, as I had trouble hearing for days afterward. But some coworkers brought me fruit, which by then Jews were no longer allowed to buy." Hansi earned twelve Reichsmarks a week. He kept one Reichsmark for himself, which afforded him two movie theater tickets. He needed fifty pfennigs for a weekly tram pass. He gave the remaining ten and a half Reichsmarks to his mother.

The woodworking machines were loud and the hours dragged on, so Hansi was actually relieved when, after a shop fire a few months later, all the Jewish workers were dismissed.

Hansi writes about his various jobs with pride: "My willingness to work and flexibility have led me to a variety of occupations. For a few months I delivered fresh linens for a laundry on the Weissgerberlände. I rode a tricycle with a laundry basket on the front. The full basket was usually too heavy for me to lift, so I dragged it up the stairs to each floor. I got a small hourly wage, plus various tips. Of course, the laundry owner was officially forbidden to hire Jews. After about half a year, her courage waned, and I had to look for a new job."

"We Jewish kids experienced this period as one long and perilous adventure," Hansi writes of the years after the Anschluss. Mounting prohibitions made everyday life difficult. Jews were deemed undesirable almost everywhere and were no longer welcome in parks, cinemas, exhibitions, theaters, or coffee houses. They weren't allowed to drive cars and couldn't own radios or telephones. From the outbreak of war in September 1939 onward, a nightly curfew was enforced, and electrical equipment and woolens had to be handed over. Starting in September 1941, Jews aged seven and over had to wear a yellow star on their clothes whenever they left the house.

For him, Hansi writes, it wasn't all that bad. So he didn't sit on the park benches now labeled "Aryans Only." He still traveled all over the city, and in neighborhoods where no one knew him he went to the movies without donning his so-called *Judenstern*, the yellow star of David patch. He had sewn his onto a jacket pocket that was attached to his jacket with safety pins. This trick was rampant—and risky. If anyone reported him, he could be arrested by the Gestapo and deported. Where would they send him? By February 1941, Jews were being "resettled" in ghettos in occupied Poland. Word had it that living conditions there were bad. At the end of the year, ten transports left Vienna for Minsk, in Nazi-occupied Belarus. The lives of ten thousand Austrian Jews ended in a pine forest southeast of the city, near Maly Trostinets.

Like many others, Hansi couldn't even imagine that arrest and deportation meant death. Perhaps that's why the risk of getting caught didn't strike him as too unsettling. He probably enjoyed the rush it gave him, the challenge of passing, the thrill of staying alert and agile. Choosing to view the dangers of everyday life as an adventure could have been a protective mechanism. Or was Hansi's perception of this period distorted by hindsight? I wonder if, with these writings, he wanted to seem stronger than he'd felt at the time. He was recording his experiences for his children, after all. Was he trying to calm their fears?

Hansi had kept in touch with some of his non-Jewish friends from school, despite having moved twice since 1939, and one of those contacts now offered an appealing trade: Hansi's Karl May adventure books in exchange for parts of a Hitler Youth uniform. He strolled the streets in black corduroy shorts and a belt whose massive buckle read *Blut und Ehre*, "Blood and Honor." Once again, he got lucky, recording only one unpleasant encounter: a middle-aged man, staring at him sternly, passed by without a word. The man's yellow star was visible on his jacket. It was his father.

The space Vienna allotted its Jews to live in kept shrinking, alongside their rights. Food and supplies had been rationed throughout the German Reich since the beginning of the war, but Jews received their ration cards, emblazoned with a *J*, at separate locations. Their rations were smaller and could only be redeemed from specifically designated "Jewish shops." Glockengasse, a street in Vienna's second district, had two such shops—one for general foodstuffs, and one for dairy. Hansi found a regular, legally permitted job at the grocery store: "I went to the owner and offered my services. I quickly went from being a temporary helper to a proper, stable posting as a salesman, complete with an employment record book. I must have been about sixteen then. It was a great help to my family. First, there was always something falling to the floor for me to scavenge, and second, my family didn't have to spend hours in line in front of the shop to get food."

It's possible that my grandparents first crossed paths on Glockengasse. Helga also remembers the two shops, the long breadlines out front, the hours she spent waiting, holding her mother's hand, her sister in the stroller, and the meager rations they carried home. She doesn't remember the young man who might have served her.

For reasons unknown to Hansi, the grocery store closed down and he lost his job. So then he asked the dairy store just across the street if he could help. Could he ever! "The owner, a distinguished Nazi party member, had won the business as a reward. She must have been a simple laborer and had certainly never run a business before. She was completely overwhelmed by the necessary paperwork she had to file with the rations office, so this part of the work fell to me while she did all the heavy lifting with the milk jugs and measuring cups. I'd sit in the back office for days on end, pasting milk carton stubs onto large sheets of butcher paper, with which I'd then settle the monthly accounting with the rations office." This must have been in early 1942, writes Hansi, because the number of Jews in Vienna kept getting smaller and smaller, so the dairy store had less and less business, until it finally had to close down.

LAST HOPE SHANGHAI

When I ask Helga where she lived during the war, without a moment's hesitation she rattles off six locations—complete with street address, apartment number, and housemates. Each successive apartment, she says, was shabbier and more cramped than the one before. In April 1939, Jews were denied all tenant protections. Shortly after her father fled to Italy, the family had to leave their spacious apartment on Margaretenstrasse. The public housing office assigned them a room on Löwengasse, in the third district, next door to an elderly Jewish couple.

In one of Helga's files, which is packed with letters and eyewitness accounts, I find a moving company bill dated June 20, 1942. Helga, her mother, and her sister moved from Zelinkagasse, in the first district—where they had lived in a gloomy middle room of a railroad-style apartment—into a crowded apartment on Grosse Sperlgasse, on the other side of the Danube Canal. Her mother paid the movers 161 Reichsmarks, equivalent to an average worker's monthly wage. The moves wore them down, and not just financially. Living together in such tight quarters was also psychologically stressful. The kitchen, bathroom, and toilet were almost always occupied; Helga's mother prepared meals on a small stove in their bedroom. Furthermore, people with different habits often got in each other's way. Helga remembers a couple of farmers from Burgenland who lived next door and got up at five in the morning. The Jewish communal organization set up an arbitration board for "legalities related to daily life," and within a few months its records reflected over three thousand arbitration cases.

Mass relocation to this kind of collective housing, which was increasingly limited to individual streets and blocks, was part of the extermination process. Viennese Jews disappeared from the areas where they had previously been familiar faces. I notice how those wartime living conditions shaped Hansi and Helga every time I visit their apartment: after settling into their apartment in the early sixties, they gradually built four bathrooms for six people.

My grandparents' home is now spacious and winding. Hansi often did renovations himself: he turned the decaying porch into a dining room and set up a basement workroom where everything smelled of varnish and I always had to be careful not to get a splinter from the rough panels of dark wood. Sometimes, when I thought no one was watching, I'd sink a nail into the tabletop. The wood was soft, so it didn't take much to leave a mark. Hansi kept working, pretending he didn't notice my attempts to decorate the place.

Today there are mementos scattered all around the apartment: in the closet of Hansi's former study, where the computer for Helga's memory exercises is, or in a compartment of the dark brown, built-in cabinets in the living room, where their old medical textbooks are lined up. I find old files in a cabinet in the study, photos in the drawer of a display cabinet, and letters in a writing desk. Helga lets me rummage around and hopes that one day I'll finally organize everything. Of course I promise her I will, but not right now—next time, okay?

I find documents and now read all about how Helga's mother, my great-grandmother Hertha, desperately tried to get her family out of the country. My great-grandfather, who'd been stuck in Italy following the failed escape to Shanghai, had settled in Milan, learned Italian, and earned some money as a doctor despite the fact that Jews were banned from working. When Italy entered the war as part of the Axis in June 1940, he was interned with thousands of other Jewish men without Italian citizenship as an "enemy alien." A former hunting lodge near the central Italian town of Urbisaglia had been converted into a camp for about a hundred men. It seems living conditions there were reasonably good. The prisoners lived in the former servants' quarters, were allowed to take walks in the park, and organized language courses, chess championships, and worship services. They were even occasionally allowed short leaves and family visits. Paul set up an infirmary in the camp and was soon so popular that he even saw patients from the town's general population and received a salary. Every week he sent a postcard to Vienna. "I keep as busy as I can all day, so I don't have to think too much," he wrote his older daughter.

During her husband's arrest, my great-grandmother somehow managed to keep getting Paul's pension payments.

They were even promised to her by the "Secretary of State for Security and Superior SS and Police Chief" in June 1939. That's what the letterhead says. Instead of the usual, curvy Roman *SS*, this stationery bears the so-called *Siegrunen*, or "runic insignia of the *Schutzstaffel*"—the ones that look like lightning bolts.

Once again, Hertha began preparing an escape to Shanghai for herself and her two daughters. She already had valid visas but didn't have enough money for the steamer tickets. In December 1939 she applied for a severance pay in lieu of her husband's pension. She had calculated that the high sum of about 12,000 Reichsmarks would suffice for their escape. Her request was initially rejected, but ultimately granted in July 1940. She received a letter from Vienna's Reich Governor stating that "the compensation of 11,814.12 Reichsmarks, equivalent to three times the annual portion of the total pension, will be paid without deductions for salary payments already issued and without any other restrictions."

But then the payout was delayed. The papers smell of sawdust, and as I sort through them chronologically, I catch myself feeling increasingly worked up. Will Hertha get the money? I know how the story ends, but Helga never told me about this settlement pay. Her memory seems to consider it of secondary importance, maybe because her mother didn't make much of a fuss about it back then. Hertha's daughter Helga was only eleven. I had no idea just how close my great-grandmother had come to getting her family out.

It took more than a year for Hertha to actually receive the settlement. On August 25, 1941, she wrote to "Herr Reichsführer of the SS and Herr German Police Chief at the Reich's Ministry of the Interior" in Berlin. She had discovered that 6,474.09 Reichsmarks had been deposited into her postal bank savings account—that is, just over half the promised sum. "My shocked request now received the response that the government was withholding a total of 5,340 Reichsmarks for taxes." Her prior petition had expressly requested that "the compensation be paid out only if the sum I would actually receive would suffice for the purpose of traveling to Shanghai." If there were any deductions, she asked that they "refrain from issuing any lump settlement, and instead continue paying out the pension as before, since I would not be able to cover the cost of travel with any amount below the expected 11,814 Reichsmarks." She closed her letter with a request that they either pay out the entire sum or let her continue receiving the pension in installments.

I can feel the anger and despair between the lines. Once again the unfair system had betrayed and disappointed her. Presumably she received no answer to that letter, because until the end of the war, the family lived off that lower settlement. Their escape to Shanghai never panned out.

Nor did the other options work out: Although the family had received an affidavit to emigrate to America, in the form of a friend's statement guaranteeing they'd be looked after, they waited in vain for spaces within the set quota. Hertha signed Helga and Liese up for a Jewish community program to place children with American families, and even had passport photos taken of the two for the necessary paperwork. In one picture, three- or four-year-old Liese holds her doll, her hair adorned by a large white bow. Helga, then about twelve, wore carefully braided hair. But even that plan, for whatever reason, came to nothing.

Then they tried to join their father in Italy. At the end of 1941, Hertha, Helga, and Liese finally got an entry permit. All they needed now was an exit permit. Once again, another wait. In June 1942 Hertha's father, the retired lieutenant colonel of the Austro-Hungarian Imperial Army, sent a letter to the head of the German police in Berlin: "I am now deeply worried about the fate of my only daughter, and ask that you grant the required exit permit as soon as possible, out of respect for a decorated old officer and for the sake of his child." This, too, was in vain. On November 10, 1941, the German Reich had closed its borders to all refugees. There was no longer any legal way to leave the country.

*

In autumn 1939, ten-year-old Helga had been transferred from the elementary school in the Hundsturm area to secondary school in the so-called Jewish Lyceum on Castellezgasse, in the second district. She liked it there too—she had good teachers and made new friends. But by the end of her second year there the school was converted into a transit camp, and classes were suspended. For several months her mother arranged for private tutors to teach Helga and a friend, but gradually all those teachers disappeared on transports headed for the "eastern territories."

Money was tight, and Helga's stomach was rarely full. "If we needed shoes, it was a disaster," she says. Hertha was unable to work because she couldn't leave little Liese alone. The toddler was often ill, presumably because she was malnourished. Fruit and vegetable rations for Jews were stingy, black-market prices sky-high. But there was always someone who helped them. There was the owner of an enameling shop, for example, who gave Hertha work she could do at home, painting tinnies, as the metal badges for the Nazis' Winter Relief Donation Fund were called. He also hired thirteen-year-old Helga to help out in the workshop. It was hard work—she had to wash the heavy paint containers out in ice-cold water—but Helga has fond memories of the owner. She still recalls exactly what he looked like, what his name was, where the workshop was, and that he left her a snack every day—a roll with lard, plus a cup of hot coffee. "You must be hungry, Helga," he'd say. His family, staunch National Socialists, didn't approve.

On the side, Helga also labeled the suitcases of her erstwhile neighbors and housemates. By winter 1941, yellow postcards were being sent to Jews on the list for deportation, summoning them to report to the appointed transit camp: "No-shows subject to arrest." Nevertheless, many resisted in hopes the political situation would soon change, thinking it preferable to stay in Vienna as long as possible. So the SS changed their approach. Postcards were still sent out, but now "roundups" began taking place as well: by night, certain apartment blocks were cordoned off, and SS men and Jewish "stewards" barged in and confirmed who was to go with them. The stewards helped people pack up and hurried everyone along; in exchange for their lives, they guaranteed the deportees would arrive at the transit camp. Each person was allotted 110 pounds of baggage, and their suitcases had to be labeled with name and address in white oil paint, as if they'd eventually return. Many labeled their luggage in advance, since no one knew when their turn would come. Helga had neat handwriting, so offered her services. Sometimes she got a Reichsmark, sometimes two apples.

When Helga had time, she went to a lending library on Rochusplatz in the third district. Jews were strictly forbidden from visiting the premises—whether the library staff didn't suspect Helga was there illegally, or whether they decided not to ask, I can't say. That's where she developed her lifelong passion for books and read her way through everything available. "I was twelve," she replies when I ask whether she liked books. It almost sounds as if she feels the need to justify having spent time reading books that were later frowned upon—anti-Semitic texts, Axel Munthe's bestseller *The Story of San Michele*, and other historical novels endorsed by the Nazis. As if she'd had any choice.

To this day, she considers literature vital. She often judges people by how well read they are. For the past few years, we have traveled together fairly frequently, and since I've been working on this book, I've become the guardian of family history. She occasionally takes me along when she has public presentations as a survivor, and as we were on our way to Salzburg she looked over at the book I was reading. It was by a contemporary Austrian author, and of course she already knew the text. "That's not a bad book," she said, "but compared to Thomas Mann. . . ?" "I haven't read him yet," I replied, adding a weak attempt to defend myself, "but I've read almost everything by Klaus Mann!" She shook her head and closed her eyes for a second, as if to underline her disappointment: "You should've read him by now."

*

One evening in summer 1942, as Hertha, Helga, and Liese were on their way home, the building superintendent ran toward them. A raid was underway, she warned them—they should take off. Where to? Hertha acted fast. A few months prior she had befriended Maria, the owner of a neighborhood boutique, whose Jewish partner was stuck in an Italian internment camp. Like Hertha, she regularly sent letters to Italy. She let Helga help out drawing some of the dress patterns, and in exchange gave the thirteen-year-old a little money. When the family knocked on her door that evening, she took them in and hid them in her workshop for a few days. Afterward, they returned to an empty apartment.

In Helga's stories, good and evil often go hand in hand. The headmaster and teacher, the enameler and his wife, the

SS men and the "stewards" who were "humane," the apartment building superintendent, the local fashion designer. It strikes me that none of Helga's memories feature characters who are entirely reputable or disreputable. She repeatedly told me, for example, about the time she was walking along the quay with the yellow star on her jacket; once, a woman she didn't know came up, slapped her, and called her a "Jewish sow." "That belongs right beside another episode," she says, and goes on to tell about another time in the exact same spot when another stranger came up, bashfully placed a bag of oranges in her hand, muttered "you poor child," and disappeared. "Do you remember more of the good or of the bad experiences with other people?" I once asked her. "It depends what you focus on," my grandmother replied.

A few months later, Hertha, Helga, and Liese—then living in yet another collective apartment—were woken in the middle of the night. SS. Chaos. Fear. Screams. Off to the transit camp. People were crowded into the gymnasium of a former Jewish school on Malzgasse, with straw mattresses strewn about the floor. Gradually, they were called up for "selection," whereby the SS checked people's papers, confiscated their money and jewelry, and sorted out those destined for the next transport and those who would stay behind and wait.

And yet, under unfathomable circumstances, Hertha's father managed to get his daughter and granddaughters released from the transit camp. Although he might have paid Hertha little attention after divorcing her mother, he certainly stood by his family after the Anschluss. Hertha, Helga, and

Liese had often visited his home in the third district. Alongside his second wife, Ella, he supported them as best he could with money and food. He also made the most of his connections—when his son-in-law Paul was deported to Buchenwald in 1939, and again two years later, when he wanted to help his family leave for Italy. In 1942, he somehow managed to speak with Ernst Kaltenbrunner, leader of the SS and police in Vienna. Kaltenbrunner assured him his daughter wouldn't be sent to the dreaded "eastern territories." It seemed the threat of deportation no longer loomed over Helga and her daughters. The Nazis did their best not to disturb the Aryan population, so his wish was fulfilled—or almost.

On February 14, 1943, Helga turned fourteen. She had celebrated her past five birthdays without her father. "One's fourteenth birthday is a milestone," he writes in a letter to Helga. "As a good father, I can only advise you from the bottom of my heart: stay exactly as you are." He describes her as kind-hearted, well-behaved, smart, industrious, and "serious when circumstances warrant." Paul remembers happier times when she, their firstborn, had been the center of the family. He might now be out of the picture, but otherwise nothing has changed. "Today's dark times have placed unprecedented demands on even you, my dear, and at such a tender age. Remind yourself: this, too, shall pass; you have your whole life ahead of you—a life, I pray our Heavenly Father, full of brightness and beauty."

A few days later Helga received a yellow postcard: off to the transit camp. Alone. Destination: unknown.

Helga's fourteenth birthday had indeed been a milestone. The "protected status" her family enjoyed had a catch: it applied to Hertha's daughters only as long as they were younger than fourteen. Hertha was, according to prevailing law, a *Geltungsjude*, or "legal Jew." This category also included "half Jews," people who had two Jewish grandparents, a Jewish spouse, or raised their children as Jews. People like Hertha. Most "legal Jews" were deported just like "full Jews." However, there was protection against deportation for those deemed "legal Jews" who had raised their children as Jews or whose children were deemed "full Jews" (which was true of Hertha, since both Liese and Helga were considered "full Jews") but were separated or divorced from their Jewish spouses. This protected status also applied to "fully Jewish" children up to the age of fourteen since, on principle, deportation guidelines prohibited children from being separated from their parents. Making unpleasant scenes in front of the Aryan population had to be avoided at all costs.

Maybe Hertha's marital status had been amended in her documents, so that her papers now said she was separated or divorced from her husband—which was true insofar as Paul hadn't been allowed to live with them for years. Presumably such an amendment would have been instigated by Kaltenbrunner after Hertha's father had spoken to him. A historian considers this to be possible, but then adds that she's never encountered a single similar case in all Vienna.

So by February 1943, Helga was old enough to be separated from her mother. Her "protected status" had expired.

My great-grandmother, however, didn't even think about leaving her eldest daughter on her own. She registered herself and Helga's six-year-old sister with the authorities.

Then Liese fell ill with scarlet fever and had to go to the hospital, where she was quarantined. Their deportation date loomed, but Liese wasn't yet well. Three times a week, Hertha was allowed to visit and speak to her daughter through a glass partition. Once again, the girls' grandfather spoke to Kaltenbrunner, who determined that Liese's family could wait for her to recover, but had to do so in the transit camp on Malzgasse. One transport left Vienna without them. Then Liese's health was deemed partially improved and, still weakened and feverish, she was considered fit for deportation. Before she left the hospital her braids were cut off.

THERESIENSTADT / TEREZÍN

"I'm getting déjà vu," says Helga. I'm standing in a quiet courtyard with her and her sister, Liese. Weeds sprout up between the slabs of concrete paving the ground. One side of the courtyard is bordered by a wall and a few parked cars, some quite damaged. A gray, two-story building looms on the other side. Its facade forms a semicircle and has large, barred windows.

Helga points to the top floor, the attic of Theresienstadt's Sudeten barracks, where she, her mother, and her sister were bunked after arrival. Compared to earlier transports, the group they arrived with was small. Two days prior, on March 30, 1943, together with ninety-eight others, they had boarded an old passenger train with wooden benches at Vienna's northwestern station, transport number IV/14f. My great-grandmother Hertha had removed the whalebones from her bodice and sewn her remaining money into their place. Their luggage included a wash basin and portable bidet. Six-year-old Liese, still feverish, had spent the journey lying on the netted luggage rack. Hertha and Helga walked the mile and a half from the train station in Bohušovice to Theresienstadt; they pulled Liese along on a cart.

The departure filled Helga with curiosity—she tells me she didn't feel any fear. So many friends and acquaintances had already been sent off. By then, only about eight thousand Jews were still living in Vienna, most protected by Aryan spouses or parents. Nobody, she says, could even imagine that going to Riga or Minsk meant death.

In Theresienstadt, people slept two to each straw mattress on the narrow, three-story bunks. The latrines and washrooms were on the ground floor, explains Helga. Liese nods. She had a chamber pot she'd carry to the latrines before using them. She'd just turn her back to the other women, as her mother had told her was only fitting.

I ask them if the latrines were in the courtyard where there's now a garage, or inside the building. They are not sure and debate the various possibilities as if they were discussing some cherished place where they used to reside. I'm amazed at the pleasure they take in recognizing certain details, like the church we passed as we walked across the old market square and the barracks' striking rounded windows. One says something that contradicts the other, and they go back and forth until one of them gives in, whereupon the second admits that the first just might be right after all. Are they indulging in some fundamental human need to fill the gaps in their memory, no matter how painful? Or has their memory of this place stopped hurting?

We visit the northern Czech town of Terezín together in August 2013, more than seventy years after their arrival in Theresienstadt. The sisters were thrilled when I asked whether they would accompany me on a work trip there, doing reportage for a German magazine. I had completed my master's degree in New York a few months before and was on an internship in Berlin. Afterward, I went back to New York again for work, and stayed almost two years before ultimately returning to Vienna.

An editor at the German magazine pitched me the assignment, and I accepted without hesitation. I'd begun realizing how much my relationship to my family history had changed since I'd left Vienna. I can't remember a time when I knew nothing about the Holocaust. As a six-year-old, I eyed the showers in a Salzburg ski hotel with suspicion. I had heard that relatives had been murdered by "camouflaged showers." How could I be sure we wouldn't suffer the same fate here? Later, I devoured every children's and young-adult book on the topic with—indeed—a comforting degree of fright. As I grew older and began to grasp the sheer monstrosity of those crimes, I often awoke in the middle of nightmares where I was running from Nazis or saw my family disappear into gas chambers. Then I stopped dealing with the topic altogether, which nobody really noticed, because people often reacted helplessly when I told them I was Jewish. What did that mean? Was I different? Were they somehow complicit? Nobody seemed to know what to say, so instead they stayed silent. Which was fine with me. I was never very religious, so I acted as if the persecution of the Jews didn't particularly interest me. But the real reason was different: it hurt to know that my nightmares had been my ancestors' reality.

When I went to England for my undergraduate studies, I was able to get a little distance. Some people asked how I could live in Austria: wasn't it just full of Nazis? I felt attacked. I—who as a teen had painted anarchy signs everywhere, read *The Communist Manifesto* to my classmates (interpreting their awkward silence as emotion), and always insisted I didn't feel especially Austrian—started to defend Austria. Yes, there was a right-wing party that worried me, but the country wasn't just a bunch of Nazis. Yes, they'd taken their time with restitution, but that's just Austrians' easygoing nature. And so on.

But it was only in New York that I really began to feel like a historical anomaly—and realized I had to deal with the past if I wanted to understand why my grandparents stayed in Vienna.

*

We stroll across the deserted main square of Terezín. There's hardly anyone in sight—just a beggar asking for change. The sisters look at each other. "Give him something, Helga," Liese says, as the man comes toward us, hands cupped in front of his chest, his face worn, his clothing ragged. Helga fishes a coin out of her backpack. "It feels great to give someone in Theresienstadt a euro," says Liese. Like her older sister, she's in a good mood. We stayed the night in Prague and enjoyed dessert at a cafe the previous evening. One of my cousins has also come along, so it feels a bit like a family outing.

Today, Terezín has three thousand inhabitants. A small museum and a few plaques recall its past. Outside the city walls stands the former Small Fortress, which the Nazis turned into a prison for resistance fighters, now a memo-rial. Theresienstadt was built in 1780 as a garrison town to protect the Habsburg empire against attacks from the north and west. When the first Czechoslovak republic was estab-lished after the end of World War I, the town was renamed Terezín. After the Nazis invaded, it got its German name back, the local population was expelled, and at the end of 1941, a group of Czech Jews was brought in to build a camp they governed themselves. Some wanted to believe it was a ghetto for the privileged and old, who would be well taken care of until the end of their lives. In reality, from the very beginning, it was intended to be a transit camp, sending Jews to the East and annihilation.

To either side of the church, which remained closed throughout the Nazi occupation, stand yellow, two-story buildings with high windows—former children's dorms. Clearly the buildings were once meant to impress; today they look neglected. Plaster is crumbling from the walls, and the street nearby is full of potholes. I look at the map. When it was an active ghetto, the building on the left was designated L414, the youth dorm; the one on the right, L410, the girls' dorm; L410 housed Czech children. Helga looks around. "Does that ring a bell?" Liese asks. "I think so, yes," she says, answering her own question. But she sounds uncertain. Helga remembers being in L414 but feels the building on the right, L410, seems more familiar. The door is unlocked, so we go inside. The ceilings are high. There are cobwebs all over, pigeon droppings on the floor, and filth everywhere. As

I climb the steps, the floor creaks in front of a door. Someone has posted a missing dog flyer in the window. Helga recognizes the staircase and window and seems chipper again, but I find the place oppressive. Its current state isn't a worthy memorial to the thousands of children who stayed here, most of whom never returned home, I think—even though it was likely in a similar condition back then. But I can't quite decide what I'd prefer instead: a beautiful renovation would be inappropriate too. If it were torn down, the connection to those children would be erased. Should these buildings be turned into a museum, and the town itself transformed into one massive memorial?

After her arrival, Helga spent a few weeks in room 18 of building L414. It was an improvement over the Sudeten barracks. Here, eighteen girls of the same age slept in a room and there was an older girl who oversaw the room, as well as older Jewish detainees who looked after them and established a regular daily routine. One of the tasks of the girl who oversaw the room was to manage the bread rations received once every three days from the camp administration. The caretakers—young Austrian and German Jews, many of whom had previously been involved in Zionist movements—had managed to give the girls a sense of community, such that the roommates stuck together and didn't steal from each other. So it caused quite a stir one day when a piece of bread went missing. Helga had been alone in the room a short while before, and she came under suspicion. Everyone from room 18 gathered and Helga was questioned. She asserted her innocence, insisting that the other girls' alibis be checked as well. Indeed, another girl confessed to the theft.

"You know me, I wouldn't do such a thing," Helga adds. I nod. Still, I'm unsure. Do I really know her so well that I could confirm it? Helga was always hungry in Theresienstadt. The physical condition of hunger, where you're always thinking of food and constantly looking for leftovers or the next scrap that falls to the floor, is something I've never experienced to that extent. Only once, when I was at an adventure camp at the age of eighteen and got only one meal a day, did I feel how overwhelmingly present the mere idea of food could become. Instead of debating life's great questions, campers shared descriptions of their favorite foods. And we knew it was just a five-day challenge. What can constant hunger do to a person? Would I have stolen the bread?

Hunger determined Helga's every decision. Like all reasonably healthy people in Theresienstadt, she was assigned work. The various workshops mainly provided goods and services needed within the camp, but some worked for external clients, including the Wehrmacht. Helga started in the ceramics workshop. When she learned extra food rations were available for those doing heavy labor, she reported to the sawmill. She found the lumber hard to carry, so she asked for a transfer. Work in the mica factory, where laborers had to use a special spatula to split apart large sheets of phyllosilicate, was exhausting as well as damaging to the eyes and respiratory tract, so that was no better. Helga was transferred again, to a cleaning crew responsible for the corridors and steps in the so-called Cavaliers' barracks, the camp's sick ward. It was horrible, she says. That's a strong word for Helga, and she doesn't use it lightly, so I press her: why? "Because I was all alone."

I don't understand her answer until she tells me how, in the summer of 1943, she was finally assigned to work the camp's vast farm. In addition to supplying Theresienstadt—and its nearly 30,000 imprisoned Jews—it also fed the SS commandant's office, the Czech security guards, and the surrounding hamlets. Helga worked the fields outside the city wall alongside a group of about twenty teenagers. She wore a heavy-duty work uniform with many pockets, and leaky rubber boots she'd stuff with newspaper. The fields were muddy, and her feet were constantly wet. During the wintertime she put all her clothes on underneath her overalls but froze anyway. The work was hard, but Helga felt it was useful because the group shared a common goal: after the war, they would all emigrate to Palestine and build a Jewish state. So it was good they were learning to farm.

When the guards weren't looking, the field workers ate whatever was even remotely edible. Apples, onions, beets, corn on the cob. "We must've had iron-clad stomachs," says Helga. After the apple harvest, they secretly buried a full box for winter storage, marking the spot with stones. But months later, when they went to dig it up, they couldn't find any trace of it. They dug everywhere but found nothing.

It was easier to smuggle things back into camp at the end of each day. Helga used rags to tether turnips to her thighs and stuffed her brassiere with apples. Someone was sent ahead to check out who was guarding the gate. If it was a woman, she'd be allowed to pat down female inmates, and Helga would stealthily let the fruits and vegetables roll out from under her clothes. The memory amuses her to this day.

Helga would probably never have taken food from another person, she explains, but she considered stealing food from the field acceptable. For one thing, it was just a tiny bit from a huge supply, of which the camp overseers got much more than they ever did. What's more, she honored her own personal rule of not keeping anything she smuggled into the camp for herself. She had eaten in the field, and the fruits and vegetables she and her fellow field workers smuggled in were divided evenly among them, so Helga gave her portion to her mother and sister.

Hertha also had to work. Ten hours a day, with one free day a week. She cared for the ill, especially children, while her own little daughter was back in the attic of the Sudeten barracks. In theory, four- to ten-year-olds were assigned to children's dorms—but by then they were hopelessly overcrowded.

Liese, then seven, could neither read nor write; after all, she'd never attended school. Nor did she have any toys. So she played with anything and everything that fell into her hands—like the packet of sugar her mother had hidden in her bunk. She took it, shook it back and forth, and listened to the soft swishing sound. Then she tore the brown paper open, stuck a finger in, and stirred it. When she pulled her finger out, a few crystals clung to it. She licked them off. When she tried to plunge her finger back into the sugar, the packet fell from her hand, and its fine grains scattered across the filthy floor. This startled her, and she couldn't get the sugar back into the packet.

A few evenings later, Hertha caught her daughter with a new toy. Liese had discovered matches and stared, entranced, at the flickering little flame. Hertha asked the camp's Jewish-run children's welfare department whether there might be a supervised place Liese could stay. They said there was room in a group of disabled children. It wasn't ideal, but it was certainly better than leaving the gentle, affectionate seven-year-old girl unattended. Liese often spoke of this children's group. Along with their caretakers, they had been deported from a German city—where, exactly, she no longer recalls. She remembers their strange accents and can still imitate some of their funny expressions: "Nahh!" "Greaaat!" "Don' say dat!" Their caretakers were kind to her, but lessons were strictly forbidden in the camp, so Liese could only occasionally play with some of the other children. She felt lonely. Being separated from her mother was painful, even if she stopped by for daily visits, and she now saw her older sister, Helga, even more rarely.

Does anyone remember that children's group? I send an inquiry to the Terezín Memorial Archives. The reply: it's unlikely that Liese was in a dorm with disabled children. "Mentally ill" children were accommodated, alongside elderly and psychotic inmates, in the Cavaliers' barracks. But there had been a building where behaviorally difficult children and "normal" children had stayed.

Liese is now in her eighties. She was once a ballet dancer with the Vienna Volksoper ensemble, went on to work as an accountant, and then spent many years with her husband's film production company. She's an engaging conversation- alist, leaving everyone feeling fine after a good chat. Maybe her memory has begun deceiving her. But I don't think that's likely because as children, we tend to notice people who behave abnormally or look different. Furthermore, I'm now thoroughly convinced that the assumption the Nazi regime was rigorous about order and organization is dead wrong. After all, Hertha had previously achieved the impossible— not just once, but several times over—such as collecting her husband's pension after his escape, obtaining a "protected status," and postponing their transport to Theresienstadt. Other survivors tell of similar events. The Nazis didn't care what happened in the camps as long as it didn't cause them any trouble. Maintaining good organization implies that you deem someone respectful, worthy. In the eyes of the Nazis, Jews were worthless.

*

The day in Terezín is exhausting. We take a break in the memorial grounds' dark cafe. We're the only guests, and the only food on offer is a few pre-packaged sandwiches. As Liese bites into the dry bread, she jokes that she's never eaten so well in Theresienstadt. Then she turns serious. "Actually, this is a city of murderers," she says. Helga doesn't bat an eye, and just slightly shrugs her shoulders. "It's not the same people," she replies. Perhaps she's had this same conversation with herself before. Liese continues: "The Czech guards were the meanest." "They were all different," replies Helga. Liese is silent. The elder sister has the last word.

OVERSLEPT

"Get up! Up!" Shouts roused the inmates of Theresienstadt from their slumber one cold, dark night. It was 5:30 a.m. What was going on? Hertha jumped up from her cot and put on every bit of clothing she had, but it was still freezing. Then she wound her way through the high bunks and frightened roommates, down the stairs of the Sudeten barracks, out along the short street, and across the market square to the children's dorm. Everyone everywhere was utterly confused. They were being pushed by SS officers—otherwise rarely seen in the camp—toward one of the gates. No one noticed Hertha as she pulled Liese from bed, walked with her to Helga's dorm, and waited for her older daughter to come out. No matter what was about to happen, they would stay together.

They held each other's hands, Liese in the middle, and joined the crowded current exiting the camp through the gate. In a huge field, they were told to stop. Orders were barked at them. There were numbered boards amid the grass, around which set groups of people were to gather. Guards posted on the surrounding hills pointed their rifles at them. Were they going to be shot? Or sent to the gas chambers?

Hours passed; they were told not to move. It was early November 1943 and the air was foggy and cold as ice. Liese recalls her spine-chilling fear; Helga remembers the bitter, cold wind, and coming down with a kidney infection after having to relieve herself out in the field.

Hours later, another order was barked at them: back to the camp! Nearly 30,000 people crowded through the gates, glad to be returning to Theresienstadt. Later on, they learned that thirty-odd prisoners had gone missing, hence the roll call.

*

When Liese wakes up one morning, she's all alone. The other three-story bunks are empty, the other children are gone, and there isn't a single caretaker in sight. Why did they leave her behind? Had she done something wrong? Unsettled, she rushes to her mother, who finds out what happened. The other children have been sent east this very morning, deported to an unknown destination. Some wanted to believe that it was a labor reassignment, but the disabled children's caregivers probably guessed that wasn't the case and had likely left Liese behind on purpose.

Liese first told me this story when I was in elementary school. She'd often pick up me and my cousin, who was one and a half years older, after school. First we'd go to the Turkish bakery, where Liese chatted with the owner while we got to pick out a pastry even though lunch was waiting for us at home. Then she'd drive us home in her bright-red Volkswagen Golf. We sat in the back, eating gummy bears and börek. Back then I found her stories tragic and eerie, but at the same time they remained complete abstractions. I suspect many grandchildren of Holocaust survivors grew up with similar experiences, eating sweets while hearing stories of children who were gassed. The Shoah was omnipresent—it stayed mostly in the background, but it didn't take much for such stories to start pouring out. During my school's Christmas break, for example, the family usually went on a ski trip. Then all the adults would suddenly decide to go home a day earlier than planned, with virtually no notice. They had lots to do in Vienna, they'd say. "We're practicing for our escape," my aunt once commented. It was a joke. But was it a joke?

Liese tells me she was glad to stay with her mother again after the other children had been deported. One of my great-grandmother's roommates was an elderly German Jew, too frail to work. She managed to get some sheets of paper and taught Liese to read and write. Liese picks up two yellowed, lined sheets of paper and shows me the letterhead: "Jewish Administration Theresienstadt." "What is our true home? Every person has a home. It can be a tiny little village, a big city, or even just a house in the woods. And this home is in a country . . . and so the Earth is home to us all, because all humans live and die on Earth," one page reads. It's clearly taken from dictation. The other page is a half-year report card of sorts: in character and comportment, Liese was graded an A. She earned a B in all other subjects, apart from arithmetic and spelling, which were deemed C's.

*

In October 1944, Helga's name appeared on the list of a "labor reassignment transport." Several girls from her room were also listed, so Helga wasn't overly worried. There were even rumors that there would be more to eat in the other camp. Hertha was suspicious, but she didn't see any way to prevent being separated from her older daughter.

Early in the morning on the day she was to be deported, Helga reported to the large hall of the Hamburg barracks. Two thousand people were being lined up by number and sent in groups to the trains waiting in front of the massive yellow building. Helga and her heavy backpack were far behind, toward the rear. Her transport number was 1680, so it would take hours before it was her turn to get on the train. The weight of her bag cut into her shoulders, and the constant commotion, bad air, and hunger sapped all her strength. She looked around. SS officers were busy rushing people on board. People were wandering around, worried, searching for their luggage and relatives. Toward evening, Helga snuck out of the hall to find somewhere to rest a little while. In an empty room of the barracks, she discovered a cot and tattered straw mattress. She lay down and immediately fell asleep.

When she woke up, the trains had left.

Helga then reported to the administration. No problem, they said; the next transport would be leaving shortly. By autumn 1944, trains ran almost daily. More than 18,000 people were deported from Theresienstadt to the extermination camp at Auschwitz. Since January 1942, 70,000 had already been deported from the transit camp.

Hertha remained suspicious. She didn't want to leave her daughter alone, so she, too, reported to the administration: she and Liese would go with Helga. That was what she had done in the spring of 1943, when Helga was to be deported to Theresienstadt on her own. That would not be permitted, she was told. Her two daughters could go, but she herself could not. Hertha knew Kaltenbrunner had promised her father nothing would happen to her. The transport list included many other mothers with their children. Was it really for "labor reassignment"? "Something's fishy," Hertha said to Helga. And she suggested Helga again try to slip out of the "sluice gate," as the loading bay was called, without getting noticed. Nobody would pay particular attention to a fifteen-year-old girl by herself. Once again, Helga was assigned a high transport number. And, once again, she successfully snuck off.

My great-grandmother must have realized how unlikely it was that they'd be so lucky again. She decided to speak to the head of the farm where Helga routinely worked. He, too, was an SS member, but also had the reputation of not exploiting his laborers—it was said he didn't work them to the bone. There is no record of how she got to him, how the conversation went, or how exactly she managed to convince him. We only know the outcome: from then on, Helga was deemed irreplaceable in the fields, and therefore wasn't to be deported. By then only a few people were left in the camp. A few days later, on October 28, 1944, the last train left Theresienstadt for Auschwitz.

*

If you ask Helga about her time in Theresienstadt, she says she'd never have survived without her mother. It wasn't just Hertha's presence of mind that saved Helga from deportation. When her daughter was hungry, Hertha gave her the last piece of bread. And she encouraged Helga to take good care of herself using the washbasin and portable bidet she'd brought along to Theresienstadt, so they could stay as clean as possible. That was how she'd been taught at the boarding school for officers' daughters, and she never gave those habits up. And of course her daughters were the same way. Helga proudly proclaims she was one of the few to never have lice, the dangerous parasites that transmitted typhoid fever. But even she was powerless against bedbugs; she'd clean the wooden frame of her cot with boiling water to get a few days' reprieve, but soon after they'd be back.

When I think of Helga, I can smell her—a mixture of lightly perfumed skin cream, baby powder, and toothpaste. She passed this impeccable hygiene on to subsequent generations, safeguarded like an inheritance from her mother. "How often do you change your sheets?" she wanted to know when I returned to Vienna and, after staying with my parents the first few months, moved into an apartment of my own. "Every week, right?" I didn't give a direct answer: "It depends . . ." She stared me down, quite stern, so I tried to shift focus. I told her I'd had classmates in college who didn't change their sheets all semester. Helga wrinkled her nose and quickly changed the subject.

When we grandchildren were small enough that three or four of us fit into the tub together, Helga ritualistically oversaw our evening bath. "When did you last clean behind your ears?" she'd ask. Whatever our answer, she would insist on checking and express disgust if we weren't up to par. "And your neck is filthy!" She'd take a washcloth, wet it, and scrub us down.

Hertha and Helga had a close mother-daughter relationship, but they still disagreed every now and then, even into old age. At the camp, Helga was the most important person for Hertha: "You're the one who has to replace my mother, husband, and friends," Hertha wrote in a letter to her daughter on the occasion of Helga's fifteenth birthday, in February 1944. She admits she scolds Helga a little too often but goes on to write that she only does it so others won't reprimand her for not raising her daughter right. I've read that a formal tone reigned over most conversations in Theresienstadt. It was customary among Austrian and German Jews to address one another formally and use people's full academic or other honorary titles. Hertha was under enormous pressure. She worried about her children's future, and rumors about the fate of those who'd been deported must have weighed on her. The more pressure people endure, the more they argue, because fear and insecurity wear our nerves down. Staying in contact with the outside world helped Hertha a little: letters and small parcels from her father and his wife routinely arrived from Vienna. Her husband, Paul, had also regularly written her postcards from the Italian camp, but since mid-1944 she hadn't gotten any more messages from him. Their shared acquaintances in Vienna hadn't heard from him either.

PEPI

I've yet to find the answer to a key question. I reread Hansi's notes, listen to an interview he did with a historian in the late 1980s, ask my grandmother, my aunt, and all relatives Hansi and Pepi spent a lot of time with—but just how Josef Feldner, whom everyone called Pepi, and the Bustin family met and became friends remains a mystery. I've only found one potential connection: from 1921 to 1938, Pepi worked as a doctor in Viennese middle schools and other so-called special schools, including the high school on Radetzkystrasse, in the third district, where my ten-year-old grandfather Hansi took classes for a brief nine months before dropping out in May 1936.

Josef Feldner was born in Vienna in 1887 and came from a liberal, Catholic family of merchants. He studied medicine and worked on the special education ward of the University Children's Hospital, where he spent a lot of time observing "mentally abnormal" children and discussing their cases. He also worked as a school doctor, treating children and adolescents of all different social classes. Pepi believed children with abnormal behavior were somehow developmentally "stuck," and could heal themselves if they were asked the right questions and adequately listened to.

I suspect Hansi and Pepi met at school. Perhaps Hansi was a challenging case? Records clearly show he was a reluctant, imbalanced student but also intelligent and full of energy. Perhaps Pepi paid Hansi a house call, met his parents and younger brother, advised them as they discussed switching schools, and then followed up on the boy's progress. This would seem to fit with Pepi's routine approach to the job, as later described by the well-known pediatrician Hans Asperger on the occasion of Pepi's seventy-fifth birthday in 1962: "He understands countless children's personalities in the most intimate detail, having followed them through the years, attended conferences on a regular basis, worked in middle schools to advocate for such children, and having often found a way when cases were considered hopeless." Asperger went on to say he "tirelessly pursues his cases, year after year, doing research within the family (for those who know to pose questions as he does, all doors open). He follows the lads on their respective paths, sometimes into the darkest realms . . ."

Pepi had four brothers and two sisters. Between the two world wars he, his siblings, and both Jewish and non-Jewish friends formed an intellectual circle. All agreed: they were against Hitler and the Nazis. In the first months of World War II, as the situation for Jews in Vienna rapidly deteriorated, Pepi hid potatoes in his briefcase to give to Jewish acquaintances he visited, says Hansi. He also saw the Bustins. By then, merely being friends with Jews was punishable by several months' imprisonment at a concentration camp.

In 1941 Vienna's Jewish families gradually began disappearing on transports to the "eastern territories." Hansi's was one of the last families left. As an educator employed by the city, most recently at an orphanage, my great-grandfather was considered "indispensable," and his deportation was repeatedly postponed—until mid-1942, when the orphans were deported. That September, the family received the notorious yellow postcard. I searched through the papers Hansi and Helga kept, but never found that card. Consulting the curator of an exhibition on the transit camps where one such card is on display, I'm told very few exist anymore. They were sent from the Central Office for Jewish Emigration: "You are to report on ____ at ____ with your relatives ____ and luggage (max. weight 50 kg per person) to Vienna's second district school, Kleine Sperlgasse 2a. No-shows subject to arrest."

Was there a way out? All their attempts to emigrate had failed. Since the United States had entered the war in December 1941, they had no more hope of being selected by lottery for a spot within the quota. They'd had no news of Frieda, Rosa's twin, who had been living in the United States since November 1939, nor of her older sister, Sophie, who had been deported to Minsk a few weeks prior. That's the situation Pepi found the family in.

Had Pepi already considered it beforehand, or did he spontaneously decide to make the offer? Did he like Hansi because he saw him as a kindred spirit, or was it just sheer coincidence he made the proposal to Hansi's parents and not some other Jewish family? The war couldn't last much longer, Pepi told my great-grandparents. He had been listening to British radio in secret and knew that the Wehrmacht had suffered its first defeats in the Soviet Union that winter, and that the Royal Air Force was bombing German cities. He proposed that the parents report for the summons, but he would take in the two boys, fourteen and sixteen at the time. Pepi was unmarried and had room in his apartment on Neubaugasse, in the seventh district of Vienna. In just a few months, it would all be over and they'd be together again.

The parents were undecided. Two relatives had been arrested a few months before, for attempting to go into hiding as Aryans. They were deported then and there, and no one had heard from them since. They'd certainly face harsh punishment if discovered, a bleak fate they didn't want their sons to share. But then what fate awaited in Theresienstadt? "Censored postcards from the camp had reached Vienna—why, you could even send parcels to Theresienstadt. Things couldn't be all that bad there," Hansi noted. "The situation in Vienna was already so grim that people thought going anywhere else could only be an improvement." Would the authorities go looking for the boys if their parents reported to the transit camp without them? And how would Pepi take care of two teenage boys?

Even Hansi can only speculate about the thoughts that must have swirled through his parents' minds back then. They never discussed it with him, and he never learned how they came to their decision, which he calls a Solomonic solution: they took the younger son with them, and the older one stayed behind. "Nobody knew which of us would walk the more dangerous path." Perhaps they thought he was more apt to successfully face the challenges of living in hiding. After all, he never had been one to follow the rules.

By ten o'clock in the morning on September 28, 1942, the apartment on Konradgasse, in Vienna's second district, was empty and silent. Seventeen people had shared its three and a half rooms; one after the other, they had all been deported. The only things in the room were Moritz, Rosa, and Herbert's packed suitcases, labeled in white oil paint with their name and address. A few days before, Hansi had brought his belongings and the few remaining family objects—photos, some of his brother's drawings—to Pepi's apartment. "We were all too wound up to bid one another a heartfelt farewell. I didn't know what to expect at Pepi's, and my parents were trying to deal with their suitcases and impending departure into an unknown future. At the very last moment, everything happened so fast. We only had time for a short hug, a quick good luck wish, and then I was out on the street." Hansi paused in the doorway to take off his jacket pocket with the yellow star. Then he turned the corner onto Taborstrasse, hopped on the tram, and headed to Pepi's.

*

As I read the diary of Anne Frank, I compared what I knew about Hansi's time in hiding with her situation—a German girl hidden for two years in an apartment in the rear courtyard of a building in Amsterdam. A revolving bookshelf provided the only access to Anne's hideout; in order to get to Hansi, all you had to do was ring the bell of a nineteenth-century apartment building on Neubaugasse. Pepi's place was on the third floor. Anne never left her narrow rooms, but Hansi was constantly out and about. What did the word "normal" mean to Jews living in hiding?

In Austria, about a thousand people survived for more than a year in hiding during the war; in Germany there were about five thousand. Their accounts indicate that the degree of confinement Anne Frank and her family stuck to was rare. It was more common for people to change their identity, which is why many survived thanks to false papers and other counterfeit IDs. Many people had to move rather often because staying in one place for too long was dangerous. One survivor reported having sheltered in twenty-two different places over the course of two years; another referred to over sixty different spots, including abandoned suburban train cars and empty basements. Seventeen-year-old Hansi was one of the rare exceptions: he stayed on Neubaugasse for so long he settled into a daily routine.

Each morning, he would get up late, prepare some *Kramperltee*—an herbal tea made with dried apple skins and herbs—and then go to the apartment door and just listen. He was lucky when it came to the other tenants. The building superintendent was old and had failing eyesight, rarely left her apartment, and always kept the curtains drawn on the lookout window commonly found in buildings of that era. One or two neighbors were Nazi party members, but they weren't fanatics. Pepi was friends with the owner of the little grocery shop on the ground floor. Even so, Hansi avoided others as much as possible and ventured out of the apartment only when no one could be heard in the stairwell. If he happened to run into neighbors or visitors, he'd scurry past without saying a word. In the big city, that wasn't unusual. The war, food shortages, and concern for fighters on the front kept everyone preoccupied, writes Hansi, so virtually no one greeted anyone they passed.

He spent his late mornings in a lending library on Burggasse. Pepi rarely read novels, writes Hansi, hence he couldn't expect any recommendations there. So he ended up reading German nationalist "blood and soil" books, novels we'd now call chick-lit, Friedrich Schiller, and Wild West stories. I wish I could ask him if he liked those books. His answer would probably resemble my grandmother's: I had no choice.

Both remained avid readers for the rest of their lives. The shelves of their apartment are crammed to the ceiling with a broad range of books, with classics of German literature next to tattered detective novels, medical reference books next to twentieth-century war histories. Hansi's nightstand was always piled high with books and magazines, a stack that was sometimes several feet deep.

For lunch, Hansi and Pepi would meet in one of the nearby taverns. Because Hansi had no ration cards, he ate the so-called *Stammgerichte*. Since 1939, by law, Viennese eateries had to include a nonrationed dish on the menu; it was usually meager—a thin soup, root vegetables, or potatoes in an herb sauce—but if he ate at several places in a row, he could partially sate his hunger. The two then went home and had an afternoon nap. Keeping the apartment tidy was Hansi's job, which he did in the afternoons. He washed his clothes in a large pot on the gas stove and rinsed them out in the bathtub. Darning his socks was virtually part of his daily routine since the yarn was weak and quickly tore.

How did Hansi get new garb without a clothing ration card? Did he suffer from vitamin deficiencies because of his poor diet? Was he ever seriously ill? The poverty they experienced is never directly apparent in Hansi's notes. Instead, he remarks that almost everyone suffered such hardships.

Each afternoon, Hansi brewed another pot of *Kramperltee* and sat down with Pepi at the dining table. Hansi notes that he could talk to him like no one else. Pepi never spoke much. Instead, he would ask the right questions and then attentively listen, looking at the young man across the table with his intense eyes.

They discussed religion, for example. Pepi had spent six months at seminary as a twenty-two year-old, much to the surprise of his Catholic but not especially observant family. The idea had just come to him; later on, he couldn't really say what had fascinated him about it. But celibacy, among other things, wasn't for him. Many evenings, he would slip out to rendezvous with women, using safety pins inside his coat to hide his cassock. When Pepi's clandestine visits with prostitutes in Vienna's Prater park were discovered, he left the seminary.

Pepi became an atheist and encouraged Hansi to think about what religion meant to him: "During our first few discussions, as I rummaged through my various unformulated thoughts on the topic, Pepi never laughed at my naïveté. Pepi wasn't one to dismiss anyone as stupid or ignorant." Hansi's family had celebrated the main Jewish and Christian holidays, and wasn't very devout, but also didn't question tradition. With the Anschluss, Judaism had become something they were persecuted for; in the subsequent struggle for existence, rituals lost their meaning. By the time Hansi turned thirteen, in October 1938, organizing a bar mitzvah was out of the question.

Is there a god? "My childish worldview—in which God was still an elderly, dignified gentleman with a long, curly white beard, holding his generous and protective hand over the devout believers who prayed to him—was gradually replaced with a more rigorous, scientific, deterministic framework in which prayers and rites assumed the importance of meditative, relaxing exercises for simple minds." Hansi later writes that, for him, Judaism became the "gene pool" that had apparently supplied most of his genetic makeup. "The fact that many people from this gene pool still cling to the fiction of a Jewish God does not mean I have a commitment to do the same."

Hansi loved it when Pepi would tell him about what went on in the military hospital. Pepi had volunteered for the Wehrmacht in 1941, and during the war, he had worked in two different hospitals, treating wounded soldiers who were no longer in critical condition. What did Pepi—a staunch pacifist and Nazi opponent—want with the Wehrmacht? It was considered a good place for dissidents because, as long as you didn't want to climb the career ladder, your politics didn't matter. Pepi was popular with his colleagues and provided his services there each morning without attracting undue attention. While working on the ward, he also managed to get his hands on an empty paybook, which he knew could be useful as a false ID for Hansi. The police were constantly on the lookout for deserters, so Hansi was particularly vulnerable as a young, visibly healthy man; hardly anyone suspected there were any Jews in Vienna anymore.

Pepi and Hansi didn't manage to fill the paybook with the right stamps, but Hansi always kept it in his breast pocket anyway. He had sprinkled pepper between the pages—an attempt at self-defense I find quite touching; using pepper as a weapon feels symbolic of the unfair fight the two of them were waging against the regime.

Hansi was interested in the medical cases, especially since Pepi explained them in lay terms he could understand. Pepi took him seriously, and Hansi learned without even noticing. As he later described it, "Pepi was a fount of knowledge, pouring information from a wide range of fields into my head . . . He was always teaching me, but in a subtle, completely unobtrusive way. I had had almost no formal education. The meaning of every foreign word, whether of Latin or Greek origin, was dissected and explained. My intellectual life began on Neubaugasse, with Pepi."

At some point, it seems, he hit a wall. They had run out of visual material, and Pepi sensed that Hansi had to see things for himself, in a hospital. What could he do? Right then and there, Pepi took Hansi along, introduced him to his colleagues as his medical assistant, had him accompany him on his rounds, and even let him help out. "Take his pulse, please," Pepi would say to Hansi, addressing him formally, as he would a professional peer. He did it all with such calm self-assurance that no one suspected who the hospital's young new arrival actually was.

For a while Hansi even went to psychology lectures at the University of Vienna. Pepi knew the professor and trusted him. How long Hansi attended, what excuse he had arranged in case someone asked for his student ID, whether he enjoyed it—Hansi's notes don't answer such questions.

*

Why did this man save me? For the rest of his life, Hansi tried to answer that question. Hansi's autobiographical jottings don't give a conclusive answer but do offer a few hints. For example, Pepi was often able to ignore imminent danger. After completing his medical studies in 1915, he was sent off to the Italian front. The lice infestation he and his comrades suffered got so bad that he decided to prepare a steaming bath—while under continuous enemy fire. Later on, when he was awarded a medal for his bravery, he joked he'd received it for a hot soak in the tub.

Josef Feldner, 1930s.

Pepi's work was always more important to him than his income or reputation. Viennese physician Hans Asperger, who later became famous worldwide for his work on the developmental disorder named after him, described Pepi as a significant teacher, whose appearance and demeanor impressed him: Pepi was over six feet tall, lean, and had a narrow face whose bright eyes emitted a "piercing gaze." "In 1931, I was a young medical assistant working at the infirmary of the Children's Hospital when I saw him for the first time," Asperger wrote on Pepi's seventy-fifth birthday. "A child was admitted who had stuck dozens of needles into his own skin; they were discovered almost by accident during a checkup. Feldner came to see the child." Asperger had already prepared a statement on the case, hoping to impress Pepi. "But all my preconceived notions fell away after he posed just a few questions to the boy (I was amazed how he phrased his questions, so instructively, quite the opposite of the stereotypical psychiatric formulations I'd been taught). After making a few keen observations about the boy's appearance and behavior, he left. And he always left me thinking."

Although Pepi participated in the weekly roundtables at the Children's Hospital, where special cases were discussed, he was never a full-time employee—he was there as a volunteer. He lived mainly on his poorly paid job as a school doctor. He didn't mind wearing threadbare clothes and, when money was tight, eating nothing but cornmeal for weeks on end. He had a high pain threshold and could ignore discomfort for a long time. He once walked around for days with a nail protruding into his shoe, but he only tended to it once the cut it made on his foot became an open wound.

Over the course of decades, Pepi took detailed notes on about 20,000 patients he'd studied, but he published little and never became a renowned scientist. His only book, *Pediatric Developmental Psychiatry: The Construction and Disintegration of Personality*, wasn't published until 1955. A purple plastic laundry basket in the bottom of a wardrobe in my grandparents' apartment, filled to the brim with brittle paper folders, contains Pepi's life's work. I take it out, dust it off, and crack open the first file on top. It contains case histories of children and adolescents he looked after, most of whom must be very old or no longer alive today. For a moment, I think about trying to track down some of his former patients and see what became of them. Did they remember Pepi? But then I dismiss the idea out of hand. In his will, he expressly stated that his papers were to remain confidential, protected under physician-patient privilege.

When Pepi finally established his own medical practice, he had less and less time for keeping his cherished records. What did he do in order to have more time? He faked graffiti on his doorsign that read "Incompetent Doctor." This anecdote, recounted to me by a relative, fits my gradually emerging picture of Pepi. He was a quiet, shy loner who remained unmarried his entire life. He liked to share a bed with the women who constantly circled him, but none of his affairs ever turned into serious relationships.

In Hansi's notes, I read that Pepi had a curious relationship to risk-taking. He liked to gamble, but years would go by between casino visits. When the mood struck, he would go every day, playing high-stakes games at several tables simultaneously, excitedly bustling back and forth. At times he would forget what he had bet where, and the croupiers would remind him. His visits were usually short, and he seldom stayed longer than half an hour. One time he went to the casino because he needed money to pay for ham he'd bought on the black market. It cost him three months' salary, about 600 Reichsmarks. He had promised to pay the next day, so with his remaining cash, 100 Reichsmarks, he had gone to the casino in

Baden, just south of Vienna. Shortly thereafter he'd won 600 Reichsmarks, and he went home. "I have a particularly vivid memory of it, because it fit perfectly into the extended, lucky winning streak we enjoyed over the years," Hansi writes. "I can't say what Pepi would've done if he had lost that bet."

Hansi also mentions Pepi's unwavering, apparently contagious optimism. Several times a day they listened to the German-language BBC station. Pressing their ears to the radio speaker, they followed the news from the front lines, listened to Thomas Mann's voice, and heard about the resistance in the occupied territories. Pepi never doubted what he had said to Hansi's father back in the summer of 1942: within two months, the war would be over.

Pepi had no enemies, writes Hansi, and no one wished him ill. His effect on others was positive: his restrained, self-deprecating nature and attentive listening skills meant even strangers ended up entrusting him with the most intimate details of their lives. Many responded much like the boy from the children's hospital with the needles under his skin, and they opened right up.

Pepi made no secret of the fact that he rejected Hitler and his ideologies. Hansi writes that about a hundred people from Pepi's social circle knew about the doctor hiding him. I marvel upon hearing such a high number. Historians estimate that, on average, for every single Jew who was saved, seven people were involved. Pepi couldn't have saved Hansi all by himself. Family, friends, and acquaintances who disapproved of the regime—but didn't dare endanger themselves directly—supported him with food, little gifts, and, above all, their silence: they were grateful he made it possible for them to calm their own consciences.

One couple Pepi was friends with lived in an attic apartment near the Naschmarkt, in Vienna's sixth district. The man had supported the Christian government, and when the Nazis seized power, he was sentenced to a year in prison—a year he spent befriending his Jewish cellmates. After his release, he worked as a bookkeeper in a hardware store. The couple's only son was drafted into the Wehrmacht, and he was reported missing soon after. Several times a month, Hansi and Pepi visited the couple, who gave them rationed goods they could exchange on the black market. They sometimes stayed until so late at night that their hosts had even given them a house key, so the couple wouldn't have to go downstairs to lock the door behind them.

The owner of the little ground floor grocery shop in their building on Neubaugasse was also a friend. After the Allies landed in Normandy in the summer of 1944, Pepi decided to prepare a feast. He waltzed into the shop and excitedly shouted: "The English radio said . . . " whereupon the owner's steely gaze and everyone else's sudden silence shut him right up. You could be sent to prison for listening to enemy radio stations, and spreading such news could warrant the death penalty. But nobody turned Pepi in.

Pepi might have been a loner, but he wasn't lonely. He was close with his siblings. Their father had run a wholesale business, and they had all endured his severe temper. As children, they were often banished from the dinner table for negligible infractions of his house rules—all seven of them could often be found in the kitchen, eating with the help. By the time Hansi met Pepi, his father had already died, and his mother had moved to Langenzersdorf, on Vienna's northern outskirts. The siblings gathered there each week for Sunday tea. Pepi invited Hansi along, so he could meet his family. Hansi liked the visits, which reminded him of his own child-hood. Not just that, but sometimes they even had real coffee, brewed from freshly ground beans. Such a rare delicacy was savored one tiny sip at a time. After refreshments, the siblings filled a backpack with food they had bought on the black market for Pepi and Hansi.

During one such Sunday gathering in the winter of 1942, one of Pepi's four brothers told him some Gestapo officers had searched his home in Langenzersdorf. They suspected he was hiding a Jew. Who could have tipped them off? Would they continue their search and realize they had gone after the wrong brother? The situation was tense. Certainly Hansi and Pepi had discussed what they would do if the Gestapo came to the apartment on Neubaugasse. Did Hansi offer to take off and try to go it alone? Did Pepi look for potential hiding places in the attic or basement? It seems Pepi's confidence prevailed once again: clearly the officers were incompetent, the whole thing would soon fall through the cracks. Hansi mentions this episode only briefly in his notes.

As a precaution, however, they decided Hansi wouldn't come to the family gatherings for the time being. The journey had become too dangerous. A few weeks earlier, a military patrolman on the train had asked for Pepi and Hansi's papers. Pepi pulled out his own ID and struck up a conversation, explaining that his absent-minded nephew had regrettably forgotten his papers at home today, but they didn't want to miss the train, otherwise they'd be late for family dinner . . . the patrolman brushed it off with a wave of his hand—but encouraged the young gentleman to pay better attention next time. *Heil Hitler*.

Months passed, Hansi remained vigilant, the Gestapo didn't come. Had no one ever suspected Pepi of anything? I call up his wartime district file in the Austrian State Archives, wherein local party officials recorded their political assessment of him. Such files were commonly kept on people working in public sector posts. In the spring of 1940, the National Insurance Institute had investigated Pepi. No cause for concern: he had always worked for the government and was especially kind to the needy. In April 1944 he applied for a position as medical officer with the fire department: although he had not actively worked for the party, no dissenting attitude had been observed, the anonymous reviewer wrote. From a political point of view, no cause for concern.

*

Over the years, Pepi and Hansi had two roommates in the apartment on Neubaugasse: when Hansi arrived in September 1942, Pepi's nephew Franzl was already living there. Franzl was from Styria and was studying medicine in Vienna—while wearing his Wehrmacht uniform. In 1940 he had served in the Western campaign and was then ordered to complete medical training as quickly as possible. Franzl was everything but an impassioned soldier; he preferred to lie about reading philosophy, listening to Bruckner, and going to church every Sunday. According to Hansi's notes, he was somber and "mystic-beatific." His intellectual mien was ill suited to the times: "The war and current situation in the homeland called for skilled, sociable people who could quickly adapt to a variety of situations. Moral convictions and religious beliefs were a hindrance and could lead to difficulties with one's military superiors. Franzl wasn't chummy, could never be a suitable confidant, certainly couldn't tell a dirty joke, and had most definitely never gone out and gotten drunk with anyone."

Pepi, the atheist, noted his devout nephew's earnest demeanor with a touch of irony. Hansi and Franzl didn't have much in common, but they were just a few years apart in age and actually got along quite well. While the dutiful student went to class each morning, Hansi slept. Each evening, they would meet up again at home, have long conversations, and share Franzl's food rations.

After graduation, Franzl was sent straight back to the front. Shortly before the end of the war, he was supposedly captured by the Red Army near St. Pölten. "We never heard from him again," Hansi writes.

Pepi's mother, Hela, also lived on Neubaugasse for a while. By 1943 she had become too frail to continue living all alone in Langenzersdorf, so the family decided to move her. At Pepi's there was always someone who could take care of her, so his apartment was where the entire family started gathering for Sunday tea. Pepi's younger brother, a physician at a spa resort in Baden, often stopped by. He wasn't much interested in politics, but in 1938, when he was advised to join the party if he wanted to keep his job, he did. "Just imagine," Hansi wrote, "an officer of the German Wehrmacht—and an official Nazi party member, to boot—visited his mom, who was living with an eighteen-year-old Jew in hiding." After about ten months, the situation became too risky for Pepi's brother; if anyone found out he'd been in close contact with an underground Jew, he'd be sent to the front, or worse. So their mother moved into his place in Baden where, just over a year later, she died.

The apartment was rather small for four people, but I never found a trace of any fights or disagreements. No conflict whatsoever is ever mentioned in Hansi's notes either.

NEUBAUGASSE

In the winter of 1942, Pepi was given a ticket for a performance at the Vienna State Opera and passed it on to Hansi. At that first performance, Hansi discovered two things: his love of opera, and cheap standing room tickets. The next evening, he went right back, bought a ticket for seventy pfennigs, and saw *Aida* while leaning against the railing of the fourth-floor balcony. He kept going regularly, often several times a week. He had never cared about opera before—nobody in his family had been musically inclined, either—but now he couldn't get enough. It became part of his everyday life. He was often among the first in line when the standing section tickets went on sale each afternoon.

The program during the Nazi period wasn't very different from the years before and after. In addition to Wagner and Beethoven, Italian composers like Verdi and Puccini were popular. Hansi saw *Madame Butterfly* and *La Bohème* at least eight times each, *Tosca* at least six, and *La Traviata* at least five. Soon he knew the various singers' strengths and weaknesses, and he leaned even farther over the railing as he applauded their particularly successful parts. He read their names in the printed program, which cost about fifty pfennigs, then carefully folded the piece of paper lengthwise and saved it in a folder at home. If there were substitutions, he wrote in the understudies by hand. If he didn't have enough money for the program, he noted the date, opera title, and singers of the main roles on a piece of paper and added it to his collection, which by the end of the war consisted of 117 programs.

I find the stash in a grayish cardboard folder in his old study. I slip the thin, double-sided programs into transparent sheet protectors, sort them into chronological order, and put them in a three-ring binder. As I leaf through the portfolio, it occurs to me that I just might be holding Hansi's most precious private possession from that period. The programs cost almost as much as the tickets themselves. They're like a diary, pieces of evidence proving his existence.

More than a year later, in winter 2016, I decide to go to the opera myself. I've hardly been interested in the genre since the last music class I took, back in high school. The teacher, watching us vigilantly, would have us follow the notes of piano excerpts. He'd stalk through the room as some opera burst forth from the speakers, then suddenly stop behind one of us students. If you had your finger on the right page or, better yet, the right bar, he'd move on.

Then I went off to study in England and the United States. Now I'm back in Vienna. And just as I encountered incomprehension among the Jews of New York, who wondered how my family could ever live in Austria, people now routinely tell me how inexplicable they find it that I moved back to Vienna after three years in New York. I had a job, after all—a job in journalism, and a work visa! I hem and haw and indulge in all the comparative clichés ("the quality of life is so much better in Vienna," "everything just moves so fast in New York"). Sometimes I respond by talking about the stingy landlady who refused to turn the heat up in winter, or the Jewish weekly where I worked ("for the most part it was great, but did I really always want to write about the same topics?"), or the time zone difference that made it so difficult to connect with friends and family in Europe by phone. I'd tell people I'm working on this book and prefer to be close to the places I'm writing about. I gave the same vague answers I had back in New York when people asked why my grandparents had decided to spend their lives in Vienna after the war. But now those are all just excuses. I know the real answer, but I'm ashamed to admit it: in New York I was lonelier than I'd ever been before. Sure, it wasn't hard to keep busy and constantly meet new people. I even got used to eating alone more often. But I missed the family I had grown up in.

From the uppermost standing section at the Vienna State Opera, I look out across the entire auditorium. Music lovers appreciate the acoustics up here. Perhaps both of these aspects were among the reasons Hansi liked being here. Spots in the standing section on the ground floor cost a little more too: a full Reichsmark, instead of seventy pfennigs.

How dangerous was it for Hansi to go to the opera? In the event of a raid, making an inconspicuous escape would have been impossible. My grandfather writes that no one ever asked for his papers at the opera. Was he just lucky enough to not be there during a raid, or was the opera never subject to such searches? The police checked IDs in all sorts of places and would cordon off the entire area until they were done. Movie theaters were frequent targets for such raids, which is why Hansi avoided them throughout the war. But what about the opera? Hansi writes that many performances were almost exclusively reserved for various Nazi affiliate organizations, and the only tickets sold to the public were for the standing sections. The audience was always swarming with uniformed men. Maybe that's why the authorities didn't bother with raids there.

The overture to *The Magic Flute* begins. I'm surrounded by tourists. I recognize familiar melodies and am grateful my strict old music teacher had us listen to operas like this and explained how music is such an integral part of Viennese history and culture. The thought occurs to me: I belong to Vienna, so this music belongs to me too—and I suspect Hansi felt the same. Jews were banned from theaters, movies, and concert halls on November 12, 1938. Their exclusion from cultural life meant they were no longer part of a unified whole. At the opera, Hansi belonged again. He saw *The Magic Flute* twice, on May 10, 1943, and almost exactly a year later, on May 14, 1944.

After a few weeks, Hansi noticed several other men of military age on the fourth-floor balcony, who, like him, weren't in uniform. How did they have time to go to the opera? Were there other people in hiding among his fellow regulars? He didn't dare ask. "The only interactions we had were all about music," he writes. During performances, they would comment on the singing through glances and gestures; during intermission, they would talk about the singers, the conductor, and the sets. They seemed to have an unspoken agreement that their particular living conditions and everything else that existed outside that grand building on Vienna's Ringstrasse remain cloaked in silence.

One fellow opera buff showed Hansi a trick: the ushers often didn't pay much attention to regulars' tickets, so, especially for the standing sections, they could often slip in by flashing an old ticket. It was a way to get in even if the show was sold out. Hansi used the ploy several times to bring one of Pepi's married cousins along with him. Aunt Nina, as she's called in his notes, lived in Carinthia and was an active member of a Nazi women's group. Over several months in 1943, she regularly came to Vienna for a lengthy dental treatment. And agreeing to be smuggled into the opera by a clandestine Jew wasn't her only crime: Aunt Nina adored the Jewish tenor Joseph Schmidt, who in late 1942 had died in exile in Switzerland. She had entrusted Pepi with two of his records. "She was afraid they might make a negative impression if one of the more fervent Nazi ladies popped by her apartment and happened to see them. Or that one of her children might unsuspectingly mention the records to their friends—without understanding the danger, nor suspecting the potentially tragic consequences. In her social circle, such records would have been considered too liberal, too foreign, and too Jew-friendly," writes Hansi. When Aunt Nina visited Vienna, she had Pepi play the Schmidt records for her.

How many Aunt Ninas were there—people who supported the system while also skirting it? Hansi says almost everyone violated the law to some degree, mainly to ensure their own survival. They bought and sold things on the black market, stashed supplies they had hoarded out in the countryside, listened to English radio. "I only mention all this to give you a glimpse of how afraid people were of the state police, including its own members."

At the start of the 1944 autumn season, the German Reich proclaimed a *Totale Kriegseinsatz der Kulturschaffenden*, summoning all cultural workers to contribute to the war effort. With few exceptions, opera houses, concert halls, and theaters were shuttered. The Vienna State Opera was now closed. Hansi never saw his acquaintances from the fourth-floor balcony again. I don't know whether he ever made any effort to find them. Might I be able to? I locate three people who were regulars between 1942 and 1944 and are still alive: a retired assistant director of the opera, a soprano who also gave voice lessons, and a writer.

They are all in their nineties. I visit them at their homes around the city and show them a picture of Hansi. No, unfortunately, no one recognizes him. The opera was a kind of "inner emigration," they tell me. They, too, say their IDs were never checked there, and yes, the used-ticket trick really worked. They spent their afternoons in the lounge by the standing section ticket booth, doing their homework and discussing the evening's cast. "The opera was an island of peace, an intact world unto itself amid

a war-torn homeland," writes Hansi. These elderly eyewitnesses confirm one more fact for me: the opera's regulars
included many Jewish *Mischlinge*, the so-called half-breeds
who were excluded from Nazi youth organizations and the
Wehrmacht.

*

Pepi often picked Hansi up from the opera. They would
spend the evenings together, strolling the darkened streets
leading to Neubaugasse and talking. They knew each other
so well by now that one could often guess what the other
wanted to say. Nevertheless, the conversation remained exciting: "I was at an age in which most young people—especially
those without close role models—are tormented by wildly
different philosophical ideas. It was an extraordinary gift to
have such a smart guide by my side, always there to help
me find my way through the confusion." And Pepi obviously
enjoyed it too, Hansi writes: "It must've been so satisfying for
Pepi to fill my head with his ideas."

It was a lucky stroke of fate that Hansi and Pepi got along
so well, and quite a coincidence that they had so much in
common. Their school experience, for example: just like
Hansi, Pepi hadn't fit into the established system. He was
eager to learn, but only absorbed by topics that interested
him, to the exclusion of everything else. He changed schools
five times before finally graduating in 1907 in Horn, a
small town in the Waldviertel, about sixty miles northwest

of Vienna. I send an email to the local high school office and, four days later, receive a copy of Pepi's report card by mail. He got an A only in French; otherwise, his grades were mostly D's. In mathematics, physics, natural history, and personal comportment he received a C.

The two also had a similar sense of humor—ironic, absurd, sometimes vulgar. Looking at photos of Pepi, it's hard to imagine he liked telling jokes and even kept a notebook with witticisms. He never seemed to smile. Hansi was quick-witted and sharp, but not a good joke-teller. He was said to have a penchant for childish, whimsical slapstick. Once, already in his sixties, he went to the airport to pick up a friend he hadn't seen in a long time. He had always worn his hair short, but for this occasion, he donned a shoulder-length, jet-black wig, with a colorful headband no less. A pair of sunglasses completed the disguise.

And then there was their mutual thirst for adventure— both were thrill-seekers. One evening, when they were almost home from the opera, Pepi suddenly stopped and looked around. To their left the streets were empty, to their right stood a hardware store. Not a soul in sight. In the moonlight, Hansi saw Pepi point at the store sign above the shop window, fish a stick of white chalk from his trouser pocket, and hand it to him. A few days before, they had heard the British radio report that in Germany houses had been graffitied with the number 1918—a reminder of the last, lost war, painted by people who longed for the fighting to end. They wanted in on the action. Six-foot-tall Pepi clasped his hands and gave

Hansi a boost so the store sign was almost at eye level. In large strokes he wrote *1918*.

On his way to the lending library the next morning, Hansi crossed the street to have a surreptitious look at the storefront. The number was still there. A day later, still there. The next day too. Then came the weekend, and the number remained. Pepi was annoyed; their intervention had clearly gone unnoticed. As they headed home from lunch on Monday, they went into the store. Pepi called the owner over, steered him to the door, and pointed to the sign, indignant. Didn't he know what that number meant? The man immediately apologized, got a ladder, and wiped the sign clean.

Through an aunt—one of Hansi's father's cousins, who enjoyed protected status thanks to her non-Jewish spouse and therefore couldn't be deported—Hansi occasionally got news of his parents and brother. The censored postcards sent from Theresienstadt were mostly meaningless: "Everything is fine here, there's a lot of work, we send our warmest greetings . . . " In early 1943, Hansi's father wrote that his wife had died of meningitis. Rosa, Hansi's mother, would have been forty-five. She was already ailing when she was deported, Hansi writes. He was glad she had died in bed, with her husband and younger son by her side. He adds that, as a disease, meningitis runs its course fairly quickly, and patients often lose consciousness. At first I read this as the future doctor distancing himself from his mother's death by viewing it through the neutral lens of medical science. But then I read the passage about the death of my great-grandmother again. How could Hansi have known so much about meningitis? Or did he only make that rationalization years later? No, now I understand: what I'm really reading is proof of how Pepi, ever the optimistic scientist, consoled seventeen-year-old Hansi.

Toward the end of 1943, all contact with Hansi's father and brother broke off.

*

The tavern on Mariahilferstrasse was full. That day's lunch boasted a special nonrationed dish: fish. Hansi and Pepi sat at a small table and ate slower than usual, to more fully enjoy the meal. Suddenly, Pepi shoved the remaining fish into his mouth in just two big bites. "Hurry up," he said to Hansi as he waved to the waiter and then asked for the check. He sounded nervous, which was unusual. Hansi looked around the room. A police raid? An unpleasant acquaintance? No. "What's going on?" he asked, but Pepi didn't answer. Meanwhile, Pepi paid, got up, put his coat over his arm, and crossed the room, heading straight to one of the cloak hooks on the wall. A Wehrmacht belt with a pistol in its holster happened to be hanging from this particular hook. The officer the belt belonged to was seated right there, but his back was turned to the wall. Pepi took the belt from the hook, strapped it on over his pants, put on his coat, and calmly strolled back to their table. "Let's go," he said to Hansi, and they left the tavern.

A few doors down, Pepi turned into an open entryway. In the courtyard, he gave Hansi the gun and told him to go home quickly. He threw the belt into a garbage can and went back to the tavern, where he ordered a trifle and watched as the officer desperately searched for his belt. An officer appearing in public unarmed would be an embarrassment, resulting in a strict reprimand. Someone brought him a replacement from the barracks. They asked the guests, waiters, and owner if anyone had seen anything. No one suspected Pepi.

Pepi never touched the pistol again. His experiences in World War I had left him terrified of weapons. This is classic Pepi, Hansi claims: at the most audacious moments, his internal contradictions steered him to clever decisions. With the pistol, Hansi would be able to defend himself in an emergency. At first it scared him, but he just had to learn to handle it. Ammunition was available on the black market, but finding a suitable place for target practice proved more difficult. Pepi and Hansi got a pile of old boards and stacked them against the living room wall. Hansi aimed. Three, two, one. As he pulled the trigger, Pepi dropped a bunch of pot lids onto the floor of their entryway, causing such a commotion the neighbors couldn't hear the shots.

From then on, Hansi always kept the pistol on him, even one cold, dark night in early winter 1945. Pepi and Hansi were on their way home from visiting Hansi's aunt. By the time they noticed three military police officers down the street it was late—too late. On Spitalgasse, in front of the General Hospital in Vienna's ninth district, the police were inspecting all passersby with the flashlights hanging at their chests. Hansi looked around; there were officers behind them too. They had wandered into a barricade.

Pepi reacted immediately: "Run around the hospital, pass everyone." He turned to the policemen and started waving and calling. Hansi used the distraction to sprint across the street. The moon was bright, but the hospital wall was in deep shadow, so he slunk along it. It was so dark he could barely see his own feet. At the next corner, where Alserstrasse and Spitalgasse met, he bumped into another military patrol and fell to the ground. The police tried to hold him down. In the darkness it was all a confusing scramble, but Hansi managed to break free and run across the intersection onto Lange Gasse. The officers chased after him, but they were slower in their hobnail boots and heavy coats. He heard their footsteps and shouts: "Halt! Stay right there!" As he ran, Hansi pulled out the pistol, loaded it, and shot at his pursuers. Their steps grew quieter as Hansi rushed onward. Then the police returned fire.

At the next corner, he turned onto Laudongasse and stopped behind a door. Taking partial cover, he waited for the fight to come. He reloaded his gun. The officers were approaching. Soon they would be there. He was ready. To his great surprise, they didn't turn onto Laudongasse—they ran straight ahead, down Lange Gasse, firing nonstop.

Hansi hid against the wall until the shots faded away in the distance. He was covered in sweat, his entire body trembling. Slowly, he headed up Laudongasse. Where could he go? Pepi had surely been arrested, so going back to his apartment would be too dangerous. Sticking a hand into one of his pants pockets, he also noticed that he'd lost his key in the fall. "For the first time I was all alone, without Pepi. I was seized by an indescribable sense of irreparable loss." He was scared.

His aunt's apartment, where they had been earlier that evening, seemed like a safe place, at least for one night. He returned shortly after midnight, telling her what had happened. Hansi was hard to calm down. His aunt had some acquaintances she trusted, and the next morning, she could see whether they would take her nephew in for a bit. Then she drew him a hot bath. Slowly, his trembling subsided, but sleep remained out of the question.

The next morning, there was a knock at the door. Hansi's aunt opened up, only to find Pepi, filthy and distraught. He had bad news, he began to say: their mutual friend was the victim of a terrible accident last night— She interrupted him: is he talking about Hansi? He's right here.

Amid the chaos of the shootout, under cover of night, no one noticed when Pepi just took off. He couldn't go home because he was convinced that, if the Gestapo had caught Hansi, he'd be picked up from his apartment, too. They were known for their interrogation methods. Pepi thought it unlikely Hansi could have survived all those shots. In search of a suitable place to crash, he wandered the streets of nocturnal Vienna. Then he remembered he had a key to the building of his friends who lived near Naschmarkt. He let himself in and spent the night atop the coal box in the ground floor stairwell. He chose not to wake his friends.

Everyone was deeply relieved, but the danger wasn't over. To prevent anyone from recognizing Pepi, Hansi scissored off his graying facial hair. But before removing it entirely, he tried out two other styles: whiskery muttonchops à la Emperor Franz Joseph, and a Hitler mustache.

They decided to stay away from the apartment on Neubaugasse. The Gestapo could potentially locate Pepi through the number stamped into Hansi's lost key. They only returned home a few days later, when Pepi learned that the key factory had been bombed.

Hansi doesn't describe any of his other experiences in as much detail as these two, dubbed "the pistol robbery" and "battle." And he's clearly told these stories over and over again—I remember hearing them long before I ever read his notes. In the past few years, I've even retold them myself, most recently as part of a workshop back in New York. The idea was for grandchildren of Holocaust survivors to learn how to present their grandparents' stories to school classes. I was curious, so I signed up. We spent three evenings in the conference room of a shiny office building in Manhattan, drinking juice from plastic cups and telling each other our family stories. We learned how to pick an anecdote and retell it. In so doing, we were advised to outline what happened before and after, but not to explain the historical background in too much detail. The workshop leader recommended we absolutely call people by their names, but if there were too many characters, we could leave some names out.

My story was great, exciting, and easy for listeners to picture in their heads, but it could have come from any war, the workshop leader told me. Its connection to the Holocaust wasn't clear. At first I was miffed, and defiantly compared my story to the others. But on the way home I let the criticism run through my mind again. Of course she was right. But, valid as that point might have been, did that mean it had to be corrected? Would that have even been an improvement? Weren't we trying to show how history is alive precisely because it can repeat itself?

*

In April 1944 American planes began bombarding Vienna and its surrounding industrial zones. "Emotionally speaking, my attitude toward the air raids was rather strange," Hansi writes. "On the one hand, hearing the approach of the carpet bombers felt life-threatening; on the other, there was a feeling of triumph, that my enemies would soon be getting theirs." When bombs struck a nearby side street in March 1945 and shook the building on Neubaugasse, his feeling of fear evaporated as quickly as the dust from the explosion settled: "I just had a feeling that nothing could happen to me, these are my allies coming to help, they want to liberate me."

The air raids over Austria took place mostly during the day. Every two to three days a "cuckoo signal" was sounded on the radio, and everyone knew to make their way to the cellars and flak towers—everyone, that is, but Hansi and

Pepi. Hansi wasn't allowed in the air raid shelters, and Pepi didn't want to leave him behind. Once or twice, the alarm surprised Pepi while he was out and about, and he went to a public bunker. But mostly they stayed together in the apartment. Since they had to keep quiet so as not to be detected by the air raid warden, they often just got back in bed and slept.

One afternoon when the all-clear sirens were sounding, the apartment smelled different than usual. Gas! They had forgotten to turn off the gas main, and a pipe had been damaged. How long had they been inhaling the poison? They quickly left the building to get some fresh air. The sidewalk was bustling with people pouring out of the cellars and hurrying back to work or home. Pepi and Hansi strode cautiously down the street. Hansi felt nauseated, and the older man beside him was pale in the face. Suddenly, Pepi toppled over. This gentle giant, who could silently endure pain for months on end and seldom went to see a doctor, lay unconscious in the street. His face was drenched in sweat.

Hansi was at a loss. Should he call an ambulance? They would doubtless ask for his ID. But what if Pepi was so poisoned he wouldn't survive without medical help? Then Pepi stirred. Hansi managed to elevate his torso by pulling him up from behind. Then Pepi collapsed again. He heard a roaring in his ears and almost fainted again, but Hansi pulled him back until he could lean against the wall. Pepi came to and, with Hansi's help, stood up. No sooner had he succeeded than he toppled back against the wall. Hansi's body kept him from falling to the ground again. How long they were there, and how many times Pepi lost consciousness, Hansi couldn't say. None of the passersby paid them any attention. They presumably thought Pepi was drunk. At some point, he gathered enough strength to grope along the wall toward home. Hansi propped him up. By the time they got home, Pepi seemed to have largely recovered.

THE END

In April 1945, people in Theresienstadt anticipated Nazi rule would soon end. The Red Cross was negotiating with the SS for the camp to be transferred to their oversight when, toward the end of the month, trains arrived bringing roughly fifteen thousand more people. They looked awful: heavily emaciated, half-naked, and often listless or seriously ill. They were the evacuated survivors of the camps at Auschwitz, Bergen-Belsen, and Buchenwald.

What Helga had endured in Theresienstadt over the past few years had been bad. She was malnourished, and her mother had been weakened by hepatitis. But now Helga was seeing what the regime was truly capable of. Many of the newcomers died immediately upon arrival, and typhoid spread quickly. Helga had never wanted to believe the rumors about gas chambers and mass shootings. Now she saw the truth.

Helga spent the first days of May working in a garden they referred to as the "laundry-garden" because it was next to the laundry facilities, just outside the city walls. Which gate had they gone through to get there? When we visit Terezín, she wants to find out. The archives are now housed in the Small Fortress, the former Nazi prison. An inscription above the archway reads *Arbeit macht frei*, "Work sets you free." The archivist spreads a large map, dated March 1944, across her desk. A camp administrator has used colored ink to indicate which fruits and vegetables were cultivated where. Helga beams as she bends over the yellowed paper and quickly spots the laundry-garden, halfway between the fortress and the garrison town.

On May 8, 1945, shots could be heard in Theresienstadt. The SS, which had recently handed administration of the camp over to the Red Cross, was fighting alongside the Wehrmacht to keep the advancing Red Army at bay. Back in the laundry-garden, the day went on as usual. Helga and the other teenagers tended the cucumbers and pumpkins growing in large patches lined by sheets of laminate. After a while, she looked up and noticed mounds of dirt that hadn't been there before, toward the edge of the garden. And then she saw something moving—suddenly she could make out a few helmets with red stars. When the young laborers made it clear they were prisoners, the Soviet soldiers embraced the about-to-be-liberated gardeners and they all started dancing in the vegetable beds.

That very day, the Red Army marched into Theresienstadt. Later that evening, in Berlin, the Wehrmacht signed the official German Instrument of Surrender.

At the end of the day, we get back in our rental car and drive down the road. Partway along, we pull over to the left shoulder. According to the map, this is where the laundry-garden was. We see some communal garden plots and an office building. "It must've been there," says Helga, looking out the window. She doesn't get out of the car.

*

By the beginning of 1945 it seemed Pepi's prediction might finally come true. On February 13, 1945, Soviet troops took Budapest, 155 miles east of Vienna. At night, if Hansi clambered up to the attic and opened the hatch onto the roof, he could see the light of the front reflected in the sky. He began moving throughout the building more freely and helped Pepi and the other residents set up a basement shelter. They boiled water and poured it into old bottles, baked crackers, and lugged a few mattresses downstairs. It had been Pepi's idea; he had suggested they could survive for a while if there were a siege. He introduced Hansi to everyone as his nephew, and nobody asked why he hadn't been deployed to the front. Everyone was concerned with themselves and their own fears, writes Hansi. Their neighbors were also reassured to have Pepi nearby; not only was he a doctor, but he kept them updated on how the war was going too. Presumably, he had access to Wehrmacht reports.

"It was a thrilling time of excited, impatient waiting," Hansi writes. The sounds of battle grew ever closer and became constant. In early April, German tanks appeared on Neubaugasse and stopped by the corner of Burggasse. They ordered locals to keep their main building doors open, but Pepi advised against it. He didn't want German troops setting up camp in the courtyard. The door remained closed.

The front was now just a few streets away. Hansi saw tanks fire toward the outer ring road. One evening, the noise of battle lessened. When Hansi looked out the window the next morning, the tanks had disappeared. "Suddenly we saw the first Russian soldiers on Neubaugasse, taking cover in the entryways as they ran from one door to the next, heading toward Burggasse and Ringstrasse." On April 13, 1945, the Soviets declared the fight for Vienna over. "For me, the war had come to an utterly undramatic end."

Hansi's notes on Vienna in the immediate postwar period make no mention of the extensive damage wrought by the bombardments. His tales from this chaotic, still rather risky time are quite amusing. There's the story of how he almost became a politician: In the days leading up to the Soviet conquest of Vienna, representatives of various resistance groups had gathered in the eighth district, at Palais Auersperg, and laid political plans for the future. Hansi doesn't remember exactly how he got involved. He was ordered to accompany an elderly gentleman from Mahlerstrasse, in the first district, to the palace. The man just happened to be Theodor Körner, who, after liberation, went on to become mayor of Vienna and then president of Austria. Soon Hansi got a desk at the provisional government headquarters. He took down the addresses of people who wanted to participate in reconstruction. One morning, he came in, only to find his desk already occupied—someone else was doing his job. Disappointed, Hansi went home and told Pepi about it. "It's pointless," Pepi replied, "what did you think you were doing there?"

Then there's the one with the poem. An acquaintance of Pepi's ran a photo studio, and Hansi occasionally dropped by because he was friends with the owner's nephew. "As the Russian front got closer and closer, Pepi and I had started learning Russian," Hansi writes. "I had memorized a Russian translation of Goethe's poem 'Über allen Gipfeln,' the one that ends '*Warte nur! Bald ruhest du auch*' ('Just wait! Soon thou, too, shalt rest'). One day, when a Russian walked into the studio while the photographer was out, I couldn't help but recite that last line in Russian. This simple Russian soldier, who wanted nothing but a photo of himself triumphantly posing with his submachine gun—a victorious snapshot to send back home—was completely taken aback by my lofty speech. But my recitation actually did help, he got the message, and waited until Pepi's friend, the photographer, got back."

My favorite anecdote comes from another relative. After the war, Pepi's younger brother, a Nazi party member, decided to go underground to avoid potential arrest. Indeed, the police were looking for him. Officers came to Pepi's apartment on Neubaugasse and asked where his brother was. When he didn't answer, they held a gun to his head, whereupon Hansi attacked the policemen. Nineteen-year-old Hansi was arrested and had to spend the night at the police station. The next day, he was loaded in a police pickup truck to be taken away, but he just jumped out and ran off. Back home, he and Pepi hatched a plan: Pepi would go to the police station and ask where his son was. Then they would never bother looking for Hansi on Neubaugasse, and Pepi could also accuse them of having neglected their "legal responsibility to provide supervision." At the station, Pepi worked himself into a rage, went berserk—and was arrested.

There is no record of how long he was in custody, or under what circumstances he was released. Purportedly, when a friend visited Pepi in prison to bring him some food, he asked the duty officer if he could see Dr. Feldner. Apparently he answered, "He's a doctor?" in a tone of disbelief. Never in his life had he met anyone so foul-mouthed.

*

When I ask Helga about her first taste of freedom, she talks about food. At newly liberated Theresienstadt, she had been assigned to kitchen duty. She got some money for it and was also allowed to scrape scraps of fat off the pots. She and her family couldn't leave yet anyway since Theresienstadt was under quarantine: the extermination camp survivors had brought typhoid fever with them, and an epidemic broke out. The Red Army soldiers, who together with the Red Cross and Czech authorities were looking after the survivors, built another sick ward and generously distributed food. One soldier gave Helga a can of cured pork that she devoured so quickly she felt sick. After that she was more careful. She gained weight, soon found herself a bit too hefty, and started dieting a few weeks later.

After liberation, Hertha and Helga asked survivors if anyone had come across Paul. The conditions in the camp in Urbisaglia, Italy, had been bearable, and he had been able to work as a doctor and correspond with them. After Mussolini's defeat on July 25, 1943, Italy signed a cease-fire with the Allies, whereupon the Wehrmacht occupied northern Italy. When it was reported that German troops were only five miles from the camp, a security guard opened one of the side gates. Some fled; Paul stayed. He considered it unfitting for a decorated war veteran to run away. That's what my great-aunt Liese says. It sounds heroic. But Paul may also have realized that his chances of getting to southern Italy, which had already been liberated by the Allies, were slim. When he was first interned, his papers had been confiscated.

On the Jewish New Year, which fell on September 30, the remaining prisoners in Urbisaglia were deported to a former POW camp in Sforzacosta. From there, Paul continued sending postcards to Theresienstadt, the last one dated March 26, 1944.

A survivor from Auschwitz told Hertha that he had met Paul there in November 1944. Was this information to be trusted? Others had told them hardly anyone over forty had survived, and Paul was already fifty-three. Helga says she and her mother couldn't expect he'd still be alive. In a letter my great-grandmother wrote to an uncle in Vienna on June 21, 1945, she puts it differently: "It could be that he's laid up in some hospital or somewhere he isn't allowed to send letters from." Hertha secretly hoped her husband was alive, but she told her daughters their father was dead. Maybe she just didn't want to get their hopes up?

My great-grandmother planned to return to Vienna with her two daughters but was very afraid, she continued. After all, the family was completely destitute: "I feel like one of those prisoners who's been in the system so long they're more afraid of freedom than of staying behind bars!"

Five days later, a letter arrived from Vienna. "I'm a relic (coming from Auschwitz via Bucharest). Overjoyed and reborn to know you're there. Meanwhile, I'm living with Ella, desperately looking for an apartment, and have been hired. So you won't need to rely on a pension, because I will work. How I long to see my beloved children. I send you all my deepest love and devotion. Your Paul."

Helga tells me about this letter, but only later mentions she saved it. I immediately start looking for it—an impulse she agreeably accepts but doesn't seem to fully grasp. "Who cares about these old things outside the family?" she asks. Is she just being coy? I wonder as I rummage through one of her drawers. Part of her must understand, if for no other reason than the fact that, every few weeks, she herself is invited to speak at school events about being a survivor, and she invariably fills huge halls when she appears.

I find Helga and Hertha's replies in letters dated June 26, 1945. Hertha sounds over the moon and joyously fills five pages: "We're all three out and about today, laughing and crying, not working at all, and going around town with your letter in hand, sharing this marvelous news with all our acquaintances. . . . Dearest, you write ever so briefly, from your few lines I can't glean much more than that you've gone through a lot, but have regained your courage and confidence. I never seriously believed anything bad had happened to you, but part of me had to be prepared for that eventuality because the news you were sending was so terrible. Finally, finally, our suffering will be over, and we'll be together again. I've put my trust in the forces of good and have done as best I can by our beloved girls despite my diminished strength. I must tell you, twice Helga was summoned to board a transport to Auschwitz—I pulled her out. I wouldn't have let her go alone, and just imagine what would've happened if I had come along, with Lieserle?"

She writes that she'd like to return to Vienna in early July, maybe arrange her own transportation instead of waiting for the next train, which might not run until a full two weeks later. Once they were home, life would continue as before, only better. "It must be terribly hard to find an apartment now, but please remember a few things before you commit to one: it doesn't have to be that big, but you should have room for your practice, and Helga wants her own room too, no matter how small. She's already a big girl with her own private life, so she's too big to always share her space with Lieserle. And, as you know, it's important for a doctor to have a proper office and examination room."

From here on out, Hertha wanted to do everything in the household herself: "I don't need servants, we could have at most one person to help with the heavy work, but what's heavy work, anyway, if it's for us? I would also like to work a little, maybe in some 'mess hall'? Or somewhere dealing with food service! But we won't starve to death, we've gotten through it all so far, and will continue to do so." Physically, all three of them had for the most part recovered. "We all look outrageously good, considering I had hit a 112-pound low last year, so I'm pretty amazed to have regained my 143-pound weight. Of course I haven't gotten any younger—will you still be attracted to me?"

Why does Paul write that he's staying with Ella, her father's wife, without mentioning her father, Hertha asks. Is she to read that as she fears? "I'm looking forward to seeing everyone again, but I daren't think about exactly who that includes and who it doesn't."

Helga's letter to her father includes a page so dense I can barely decipher her handwriting. I ask her to type it out for me. "You cannot imagine what your letter means to me—until two hours ago the mere thought of Vienna struck me as an abomination, but after reading it, I'd rather return now than wait even ten minutes. Tell me, would you ever have dared dream such a thing?" she wrote. "I'm writing you in a rather confused state today, but it's understandable, I'm still all mixed up from such a shock (the most pleasant shock I've ever experienced). Just imagine: you have plans for the future, which seems so grim, such a joyless existence spreads out before you, and in the background there's always the thought: What's become of my father? You couldn't even dare factor him into your plans for the future, but then suddenly—it's such a miracle, but I haven't even fully absorbed it yet, I still have to get used to the thought. I'm bursting with joy, it's almost more than I can handle, to think *he's in Vienna, he's waiting for us.*"

She jumps from topic to topic and mentions how they asked after him, in vain. "You probably remember me as I was when you left, and you'd faint if you could see me now. I won't write you about what we've been through, on purpose, because I wouldn't know where to start or how to end. But it was bad. Oftentimes we weren't full, but we never truly starved, and somehow we always got through it." She couldn't wait to hear how her father had fared. "I think if one of us talks for a week straight, we'll have said maybe a tenth of what we have to say." She asks that he reply swiftly, so they can plan their departure. "I can't believe we're now a real family again, and can build a future, and no longer have to drift aimlessly as before." She signs off as "completely topsy-turvy Helga," sends hugs and kisses, and concludes with a P.S.: "You have no idea how supersupersuper happy I am."

A week later, at the end of June 1945, the three were on their way back to Vienna. They rented a truck, and Helga remembers peering out from under the tarp toward the end of the ten-hour ride. This is Vienna? She was completely disoriented and couldn't recognize a thing. So much had been destroyed. The German troops had blown up the bridges over the Danube Canal.

Would they be a real family again, as Helga hoped? They were already, on paper at least. For a little while, they stayed with Ella, her grandfather's wife, in the third district. Malnutrition had debilitated the old lieutenant colonel, and he had died of pneumonia as the war was drawing to a close. Soon thereafter, the family moved into an apartment on Liechtensteinstrasse, in the ninth district. So much of the city had been destroyed that there was now a housing shortage, and at first they had to share the apartment with a Nazi party member—that arrangement didn't work out. A short time later, they moved to a larger apartment on Porzellangasse, where her father could also reopen his office. Just as before the war, he worked as a doctor for the police again. Immediately after returning to Vienna, he had applied for a position with his former employer and gotten his old post back.

In the fall, the nine-year-old Liese was sent to school, much to her chagrin ("Once again, I'm being forced to do things!"). Sixteen-year-old Helga went back as well, with equal reluctance, as she was put in the third year of Austria's eight-year secondary school system. She hadn't been to school for the past four years and had barely studied outside of the few private lessons she had received. She stood firm: at sixteen, she belonged in the seventh year. But you don't know a word of Latin, the superintendent countered. Helga got a private tutor again and studied at home. A few months later she was admitted to the seventh-year class, and she passed the year-end exam.

Helga says she has always been ambitious. Even as a child, in the years before the Anschluss, she enjoyed learning, and her parents and their acquaintances were impressed when she could read and write at such a young age. She had grown up smart, so being excluded from school was perhaps the most painful aspect of her persecution. Now she had an opportunity to not only get her reputation back, but to surpass it. "I decided: I'll show them," she says. For a long time, she had been treated as a second-class citizen. Now she wanted to prove that she was not only equal, but at the very top. This trait stayed with her. She went on to pass her medical school exams with flying colors. Today, she still exercises, is conscientious about her diet, stays curious, and keeps learning new things. Professionally, she always worked hard; there isn't a passive bone in her body. She is in perfect health, and on the rare occasions she gets sick, she becomes rather unbearable, complaining incessantly about how she has to cancel all her dates and how much she misses her daily exercise routine.

School was a soothing distraction for Helga. Her family's home life was more difficult than she had expected. After spending two and a half years almost exclusively with peers in Theresienstadt, she was no longer accustomed to obeying her parents. Moreover, she, her mother, and her sister were as unprepared to grapple with the implications of Paul's survival as he had been with theirs. They hadn't seen each other for six years. "He was a stranger to me," says my great-aunt Liese, who was three when her father escaped to Italy in 1939, and nine when they were reunited. "I suspect our parents had to start their marriage over from scratch too."

Helga had looked forward to seeing her father again and wanted to know all about what had happened during the years they were apart. "I didn't yet know what a wreck he was," she remarks, handing me the letter she had written from Theresienstadt in June 1945. Paul was nervous, anxious, and whiny. Every night, he had nightmares and would keep shouting "Inspection! Line up! Line up!" until someone woke him up. He was grief-stricken by the loss of his mother, his three siblings, and his nine-year-old nephew, who had all been murdered. He was hardly able to talk about his time in Auschwitz. Little by little, his family learned he had been deported to the extermination camp in early April 1944, alongside eight hundred others from Sforzacosta. He survived eleven months working on a hospital ward, supposedly in a lab where he analyzed blood samples at night. He might have kept his strength because the indoor work protected him from the extreme cold outside, or because he didn't have to do any hard physical labor and had access to little things like paper scraps or bits of flint he could trade for food. Maybe he ran into old acquaintances who helped him. At the end of January 1945, he was ordered to line up with all the other remaining inmates. The SS had planned to shoot them, but changed their mind at the last moment and decided to flee from the approaching Red Army instead. After liberation, Paul caught typhoid fever, was nursed back to health at a hospital in Krakow, and by the end of May, finally got back to Vienna via Bucharest.

Helga has a hard time describing what it was like to live with a traumatized father. "I'd say that he functioned, more than really lived," she says—but "I mustn't write it like that, he doesn't deserve that," she adds. He tried. And she is ashamed of how she made him feel, hinting that she bristled around his fearfulness and his sentimentality got on her nerves. Years of humiliation made her seethe with anger and hatred of the Nazis, both old and new. "I wanted to see one hanging from each and every lamppost," she says, grimacing, repelled by the recollection of an impulse that didn't square with her notion of herself as an even-keeled person.

She didn't think much about it in school. The other girls in her class regarded Helga as a "creature from a panopticon," she says, with a mixture of fear and curiosity. Most of them couldn't even remember ever having known a Jew. By then, Vienna's Jewish community had five thousand members; in 1939, it had been nearly eighty thousand. Over time, the distance between Helga and her classmates narrowed. Many girls had gone hungry during the war, lost their fathers and brothers, and been bombed out of their homes. Helga saw that the Nazi regime had treated many innocent people unfairly, not just her.

I, too, know what it's like to be different from my classmates. I was always the only Jew, and usually the only non-Christian in my class. Year after year, I had to explain to my peers that I didn't celebrate Christmas, a notion they found disturbing. What, no presents at all? And what about December 24 and 25? They're just like any other day? They pitied me, and I didn't know how to handle it, so I told them that, actually, sometimes my parents would give me little presents for no apparent reason. It relieved them to know that even my parents, the non-believers, adhered to the apparently divine order of gift-giving that, up to a certain age, everyone seemed to believe in.

*

"We are overjoyed to hear you are alive and hopefully healthy. Please write us immediately, in detail, about the whole family. I've regrettably only been able to get mixed reports to date. I'm afraid we've heard so much sad news that we're quite scared, but please write us as soon as you can, tell us the truth about everything. You poor dears, what have you been through?" On December 31, 1945, Hansi's Aunt Frieda, his mother's twin, wrote these lines from her Bronx apartment. She had gotten her nephew's address in Vienna from a relative.

Hansi's cousin Ilse—the daughter of Hansi's aunt Sophie, his mother's older sister—got his address around the same time. She had gone to England as a twelve-year-old in 1938, had attended a Quaker boarding school, and was now in college, studying to become an elementary school teacher. "I know very little about how things went for you all during the war, but I hope to hear from you very soon," she wrote Hansi. "Do you know where all our relatives are, and whether my mother is still alive?"

As Ilse's ninetieth birthday approaches, I visit her in London. She used to visit Vienna regularly. As a retired elementary school teacher, she knew how to handle us children.

We'd alternate days with her, speaking English one day, German the next. She's a shy, melancholic woman whose fine sense of humor still flashes across her face every now and again. "Do you know how many fingers you have?" she would quiz us. We always forgot how the trick worked, so we let her show us over and over again. "Ten!" we would answer. "Are you sure?" she'd ask, counting from one thumb to the little finger and back again. The trick was that she only counted the little finger once, and she got us every time.

In the meantime, she's become too frail to travel and now lives in a nursing home in northern London. I show her the thin, light-gray pages she wrote with a fountain pen, in her rather childlike hand, after the war. She remembers the moment she received Hansi's answer: "I thought, oh, it's the first letter from our family in Vienna! I went out to a hockey field, because I wanted to be alone while reading it. I was so shocked. It was the first and the last letter, because no one else had survived."

Ilse's mother was deported from Vienna to Minsk on September 14, 1942. She was probably shot immediately upon arrival in a pine grove near Maly Trostinets. Hansi's parents and fourteen-year-old brother Herbert were deported to Theresienstadt two weeks later. A postcard sent from the camp in early 1943 informed Hansi his mother had recently died of meningitis. On December 17, 1943, his father and brother boarded a transport to the "Reich territory." Moritz had transport number 1555, Herbert, 1760. The cattle cars, crammed with 2,500 people, left Theresienstadt in the early morning of December 18, 1943, and reached Auschwitz-Birkenau the following day. In the "family camp" section of Auschwitz that his father and brother had been deported to, none of the notorious selections as to who would be sent on to the gas chambers were made upon arrival. From the outset, however, the Nazis only planned the family camp to be temporary. In July 1944, all working-age inmates were sent to other camps; the majority of those remaining were murdered in the gas chambers.

For months after the war's end, Hansi awaited the return of his father and brother. When he heard about survivors stranded in Vienna, he would run to ask them for news of Herbert and Moritz. He finally learned that Moritz had been shot on a death march near the Sachsenhausen concentration camp, just a few weeks before liberation.

*

As I'm doing research for this book, a memorial is erected on the former site of the Aspang train station, from where most Viennese were deported. One of my cousins, as chairman of a Jewish student organization, is preparing to give a public address here on the anniversary of the November pogroms. I'm sitting in a restaurant, across the table from my mother, when he calls. Were our great-grandparents and Hansi's brother, Herbert, deported from the Aspang train station? Yes, I answer, and explain what happened to our grandfather's family: Theresienstadt, meningitis, Auschwitz; family camp, selection, Sachsenhausen. I talk fast, get all excited, and feel the exhilaration I always do when I know the right answers to tough questions. When I hang up, I see a shocked look on my mother's face. "I never knew all those details," she says.

Conversely, for me, the past has once again grown more abstract. Just as I used to read children's books about the Holocaust, I now enjoy discovering unknown details and telling my family's story. The sheer proximity and cruelty of it all has started to slide into the background. I'm often only reminded of it by others' reactions. Of course I know that a bit of distance is necessary in order to just put the story on paper. But am I actually starting to take some satisfaction in understanding the horrific logic of the Nazi regime? I carefully observe my mother's expression as I explain the role of the Theresienstadt family camp and tell her about the database in which I found her grandmother's deportation record and death certificate. "Despite all that, here we are," she says. It's our story, and it's good I tell it.

*

"For years I had hoped to see my sister again, but it was all in vain. All the wailing and whining in the world won't help, nothing can help us now," wrote Hansi's inconsolable Aunt Frieda in February 1946, after he had informed her of his mother's death. Frieda was now determined to gather her surviving family members—in the United States. She had already announced in her first letter that she wanted to send her nephew an affidavit so he could come to America with an immigration visa and forget all the horrible things he'd been through. "We want to bring you here, and you'll see—you'll soon be the happy old Hansi again," she wrote. "The worst is behind you, and you got through it. What's in store can only be better."

Her daughter—Hansi's cousin Litzi, who had fled to England in 1938 and later went on to the US—echoed the same enthusiasm. In early 1946 Litzi was a twenty-three-year-old newlywed, and regularly sent care packages to Vienna. She wrote Hansi letters all the time. Twice she reminded her cousin to contact the American Consulate. In September 1945, when he reports that he has started his last year of secondary school and is struggling in math and Latin, she calms him down: in America nobody learns Latin, school is much easier, and he has nothing to worry about. "Stay healthy, and just picture the great time that awaits you here in America!"

But Hansi didn't want to go to America. He thought it was more sensible to complete his education in Vienna: first of all, he had no money to cover the move; second, his English wasn't good enough for him to continue studying at an American university. He wanted to become a doctor, just like Pepi, with whom he was still living. Moving to America would mean splitting up. Hansi poured his heart out to nineteen-year-old Ilse in England, and she was receptive. "I completely understand why you don't want to go to America," she replied in March 1946. "Over the last two years, I've had to explain to Aunt Frieda time and again why I don't want to go to America, telling her I can stand on my own two feet, want to continue doing so, and am determined to continue doing so. . . . But you must also try to understand her point of view. Aunt Frieda is committed to taking care of us all because, of the three sisters, she's now the only one left."

HANSI AND HELGA

Facts have a way of disappearing, that much is clear to me. Hansi's secondary school? There are no archives of it. Paperwork from the period Pepi worked under the Wehrmacht? Unavailable. The documentation proving Helga's "protected status," or that of her sister and mother? We can only make educated guesses. How many people knew about Hansi's existence as a Jew in hiding? No way to find out.

My uncertainty about just how closely Hansi and Helga's recollections actually are to reality must also be factored in. Helga has spent her entire life dealing with the Holocaust quite intensively. To what extent have her experiences begun to meld with others'? Hansi's notes remained incomplete. The last entry dates from a few weeks after his seventieth birthday, shortly before he was diagnosed with cancer. If he'd had more time, maybe he would have been more like Helga. With each conversation, she recalls new details.

When she tells me how she met Hansi, I wonder what his take would have been. He doesn't say a word about it in his notes.

Emigration to Palestine was a huge topic among Vienna's surviving Jews, including Helga, who had come into contact with the idea of Zionism in Theresienstadt. On September 11, 1945, she attended a Zionist group meeting. She remembers the date exactly. A warm meal was served, and probably not everyone there was an ardent Zionist, including the lean young man with jet-black hair and a striking look seated opposite her. He was nineteen, Helga sixteen. "He caught my eye," says Helga.

Helga was there with a girlfriend, Hansi with a male acquaintance of his, and the four of them decided to get together again soon. On the occasion of his twentieth birthday on October 18, Hansi invited Helga to the apartment on Neubaugasse. They drank and smoked. Pepi was there and talked to her. Helga wanted Hansi to like her—she was impressed by how wild he was, how he bristled at the idea of abiding by the rules. When the weather improved, the group of new friends spent entire afternoons in a garden on Wilhelminenberg, toward the outskirts of the city. One time, Hansi climbed up onto the roof of the garden shed. "My heart stopped," Helga recalls. Then he just casually jumped down again.

He had another idea: Helga should stand in front of the wooden wall. Hansi would show off his knife-throwing skills; Helga would prove how courageous she could be. "I thought I'd wet myself, I was so scared!" Hansi proved to be a masterful knife thrower, and to this day Helga shudders just thinking about it.

In those first few months after the war had ended, Hansi realized his years of isolation were over, and he was savoring it to the hilt. Helga kept spotting him in the company of other young women, until she learned how to make him jealous

Hansi and Pepi, late 1940s.

in turn. She went to the Volksoper with one admirer ("a good-looking guy, but dumb as a doornail") and had another over to play chess; he ended up staying past the curfew. "He thought maybe something was brewing and asked to spend the night." Helga handed him a blanket and said he could sleep in the elevator, but the next morning she did bring him breakfast.

Helga and Hansi circled one another for nine months. Helga described it as an "on and off situation." Who decided that? I ask. "Each of us had our own sore spots," she replies. Vienna was nearly destroyed, money was tight, and Helga was full of rage over the years of torture. She wanted to emigrate to Palestine. And what was Hansi grappling with? Later on he told my aunt that the murder of his sixteen-year-old brother was the hardest blow he'd ever been dealt.

By the summer of 1946, Hansi and Helga were a couple. They took off for a weekend: the official story was that Helga was on the road with a girlfriend; instead, she entrusted that girlfriend with the task of sending Helga's parents a couple of pre-written postcards. Helga's father had been especially suspicious of Hansi from the start. Exactly why, Helga can't say. Maybe he just didn't care for him, or thought his daughter was too young.

In July, thanks to some major help from Pepi, Hansi passed his high school graduation exam. During the Latin portion, Hansi told his teacher he felt nauseated. He was given permission to go to the bathroom, where Pepi translated the text. That autumn, Hansi enrolled in the University of Vienna medical school. One of Pepi's letters to Aunt Frieda painted the picture: "He gets up at 8:00, which I give him extra credit for, goes to class, comes home at 1:30, and only has fifteen minutes for lunch, since he has to be back in the dissecting room by 2:00. In the evenings, he has to study, reviewing all the anatomical details he dissected that afternoon, so that he can continue dissecting farther the next day." He goes on: "Hans has nothing but very decent, nice acquaintances. He himself is, thankfully, still solid, and shows no inclination to rebel. He enjoys a glass of wine—an occasion that presents itself only rarely—but he would never get drunk. He attended a ball this past season, and came home at 3:00 a.m. But since he can't really converse at such events, he prefers to find a table somewhere quiet with some boys and girls and just talk the night away."

Helga still had another year of school ahead of her, which felt like an eternity. Surprisingly, she suddenly decided to quit school and instead take a shorter, six-month course to get her high school diploma—and, alongside Hansi, start studying for the medical exam. In the spring of 1947, half a year after Hansi, she passed her high school graduation exam and immediately enrolled in medical school. She had her own little room in her parents' apartment on Porzellangasse, in the ninth district, and Hansi often visited her there so they could study together. In between, she says, they would take little breaks, which particularly piqued the curiosity of her eleven-year-old sister Liese. Helga had a model skeleton that terrified Liese. The next time Liese knocked on the door to her room, Helga put a flashlight in the skeleton's mouth, turned the overhead light off, and stood the skeleton in the middle of the doorway so it would be right in front of Liese as she opened the door. After that, Hansi and Helga were left in peace, for a while at least. And Helga's plans to go to Palestine? They had vanished.

POUGHKEEPSIE, NEW YORK, 1955

The photograph in my grandmother's bedroom was taken on March 9, 1955. When the *Saturnia*—sailing via Genoa and Halifax—arrived in the port of New York, several reporters came aboard. A Jewish charity had informed them a young couple from Vienna with unique life experiences was on board. Hansi and Helga aren't looking straight at the camera but gaze off to the left. The caption underneath reads: "Also aboard the *Saturnia* were Drs. Hans and Helga Feldner-Busztin [*sic*], who came from Vienna to intern at Poughkeepsie Hospital. Dr. Helga was liberated from Nazi concentration camp in 1945. Dr. Hans said his brother and parents perished in concentration camp but he escaped when a Christian doctor adopted him." Pepi, the staunch atheist, a "Christian doctor?" Hansi didn't like the article in the least: "The newspaper really annoyed me," he writes Pepi a few days later. "The pictures show us smiling like idiots." To me, their smiles look full of anticipation, but also uncertainty.

Three years earlier, the two had completed their medical studies. Helga was the only woman in their graduating class. Now they wanted additional training in their chosen specializations. Hansi was interested in neurology, Helga in internal medicine, but in Vienna, physicians in training were poorly paid. Helga worked as an intern, Hansi was on the waiting list for an apprenticeship, and in the meantime he served as a volunteer visiting physician at the university hospital's neurological ward. Only for nighttime services did he receive even modest pay.

Beginning in 1949, both received a "restitution pension" from the state, 571 shillings a month. Helga was granted compensation as a victim of Nazi persecution, and Hansi because he was the survivor of a victim—his father. According to the second amendment to the Austrian Victims' Benefits Act of 1947, people who had been imprisoned for at least six months in a concentration camp or spent a year in prison were entitled to such pay. In the first version of the law, only resistance fighters had been recognized as victims. In the Municipal and Provincial Archives of Vienna, I read along as Hansi fought for twenty years to be recognized and compensated. It all started with the restitution pension, which he only received until his twenty-fifth birthday, under the assumption that he would have completed his education by then. By 1950 he had not yet finished his studies so, year after year, he had to submit a renewal application. It was always granted. In 1952, the social security and welfare laws were amended again and, in addition to the current benefits, victims were now entitled to "detention compensation." The sum Helga received was increased, and Hansi received some money for the months his parents had spent in concentration camps, but now he was hoping to obtain a separate victim's ID card so that the two and a half years he had spent in hiding would be officially recognized as a "deprivation of liberty"—i.e., another type of imprisonment. His application was rejected, with the stipulation that "living in hiding" did not qualify as imprisonment "according to the victims' benefits act." Hansi objected and filed a petition: "Since I had no papers, no food ration cards, and no money, my life was excruciatingly impoverished. As a 'full Jew' and 'star wearer,' I was not to be seen on the street, and therefore could not carry out any employment; hence, until liberation in 1945, I was deprived of my freedom and lived like a prisoner, in the most meager conditions. Furthermore, because I was not allowed in the air raid shelter during bombardments, I was constantly put in mortal danger. . . . Living in a state of perpetual fear, deprivation, and confinement, my health and mental state suffered greatly. Given that, during this time, my life bore all the traits of imprisonment—I suffered greatly from deprivation of liberty, hunger, and social marginalization, and my existence as a prisoner was additionally burdened by the constant threat of bombardment or police harassment—and these inhumane life circumstances were caused by the general arrest warrant the state had issued against me, I consider this denial to acknowledge my status as prisoner a serious injustice, and one that the legislature could not possibly have intended to carry out in the spirit or letter of its law."

This, too, was unsuccessful. "Strictly speaking, time spent living in hiding cannot be classified as imprisonment," was the reasoning the Federal Ministry of Social Affairs offered in November 1956. "In order to qualify as imprisonment, it is essential: that one's physical movement be restricted—either

Helga and Hansi, 1950s.

by a guard or other type of cordoning-off—to a room intended exclusively for detention; that the detainee be subject to the disciplinary authority of the detention center; that the detainee's daily routine be entirely governed by the detention center; and that the detainee be prevented all contact with persons whose freedom is not limited."

One year later, Hansi was finally recognized as a victim. Hansi didn't receive any compensation from the Republic of Austria for the years he was forced to live in hiding until 1963, eleven years after he had first submitted his application. The legally stipulated compensation was increased again in the mid-sixties. Hansi and Helga also received compensation for having been forced to wear the star of David, and for the interruption of their studies. They also received payments from *Sammelstelle A*, or "Collection Point A," a fund from which stolen Jewish assets with no identifiable heirs were distributed to survivors.

It's not nothing, I think, and discuss it with Helga. What was problematic, she says, was that it was paid out so late. In the immediate postwar period, they relied on the Jewish community's welfare services. Helga's parents' apartment on Porzellangasse, for instance, was only furnished thanks to the community's resources, and Hansi received a scholarship to continue his studies. And then there were the packages and small sums of money Hansi's American relatives regularly sent. Things seemed to be going much better over there.

Helga likes to talk about the parcels. She pauses and looks at me: "You cannot possibly imagine," she says. It's a sober assertion, and she's absolutely right. I nod. Throughout my life, my every need—and, oftentimes, my every want—has always been satisfied.

*

As soon as the war ended, Hansi's family in New York began encouraging him to emigrate. His graduation, in early summer 1952, offered an opportunity. Young American physicians had to complete a one-year internship, in which they would work in various divisions of a hospital. These internships were well paid, and there were a lot of vacancies back then because there was a shortage of doctors throughout the United States. Hansi's cousin Litzi learned that up in Poughkeepsie, north of New York City, two such posts were vacant. They paid $200 per month, the equivalent of about 4,000 shillings, which was more than twice the average monthly salary in Austria at that time. Room and board were included. Hansi applied for an immigration visa. Solely in order for Helga to go along too, they got married. The way she tells it is wholly unromantic and yet beautiful at the same time: the visa was the real reason they tied the knot, she says, but they knew they belonged together anyway.

On March 12, 1952, they signed their marriage certificate at the civil registry office on Martinstrasse, in the eighteenth district. Helga wore a simple black dress, the same one she wore at her graduation from medical school a few months later. Their group was small, she says, fewer than ten people. There was no money for a big celebration. For their honeymoon, they drove to Semmering, an hour away from Vienna, and stayed a few days. Helga continued living with her parents on Porzellangasse, Hansi with Pepi on Neubaugasse. They couldn't afford their own apartment.

*

Hansi's relatives in New York closed for the day their carpentry workshop and small furniture store in the Bronx in order to welcome Hansi and Helga upon their arrival. Hansi's cousin Litzi had recently moved to a suburb out on Long Island. She and her husband had two small children and brought them along to the harbor.

"Outwardly, Aunt Frieda hasn't changed a bit," Hansi wrote back to Vienna regarding his mother's twin sister, whom he'd last seen a decade and a half prior. "But she's never recovered from the loss of her relatives." Of the three sisters, Frieda was the only one to survive the Holocaust. She had corresponded with them up until the United States entered the war, in December 1941. I find a letter in Litzi's apartment on Long Island. On April 28, 1941, my great-grandmother Rosa wrote to her sister in blue ink on beige onionskin paper: "I'm rushing to send my swift and heartfelt thanks for your precious letter! I read it with such joy, & words cannot express how much I & all of us are rejoicing along with you!" Frieda's husband had gotten a promotion. She continued: "I was immediately reminded of how I had predicted, just before your departure, that Michel would first become a factory manager, & then bring us all over. Those words were a serious wish on my part, and I now realize a small part of my wish has already been fulfilled!... Now I just want to sincerely congratulate you on your new position, & we all hope the good Lord will bestow continuing success upon all your endeavors, & that you & yours may achieve all your goals in fine health & happiness, wherever your path may lead! As for me, I can only express an inner, more modest, yet fervent hope that I & mine might 'soon be eyewitnesses of your calm, well-deserved contentedness.'"

The very day Hansi and Helga arrived, they got a call from the hospital in Poughkeepsie. Management wanted them both to come immediately, not two weeks later as planned. They agreed to report for duty the following Monday. That Sunday, the family drove them up to Poughkeepsie by car, in just under three hours.

A few days later, Aunt Frieda wrote to Pepi, whom she had never personally met. She blames herself for not having sufficiently spoiled her nephew and his wife immediately after they arrived. She was too upset: "When I look into his dark eyes, I see his mother standing before me, and then I get so emotional I can barely hold back my tears. I get so worked up; without even talking about the past, memories that have lain dormant for years are now being awakened. I walk around as if in a dream . . . "

*

The young couple was assigned a small bungalow on the spacious hospital grounds overlooking the Hudson Valley. Ten years had passed since they had met, and now they were living together for the first time. They had a large room, a bathroom, and even a porch. How was it? "Good" is all Helga says. They were rarely home and could eat four meals a day at the hospital cafeteria. Every other night and every other weekend they were on call, a duty they usually did together: those on first call had to be the first responders in case of emergency; those on second call stepped in when the first-call doctor was already busy. It was fairly rare to get a second-call summons, so Helga and Hansi split the shift so that each could get a little sleep.

The team of interns was small—two Mexicans, two Americans, a Greek, and a Persian—and constantly busy. They learned a lot; being at the most important hospital in a city of 40,000 meant they got to see a broad range of cases. Because there were only a few experienced doctors, the interns took on a lot of demanding roles: in the children's ward, Helga treated kids affected by the polio epidemic; in gynecology she delivered newborns and carried out curettages. Hansi performed a fair number of surgeries on his own. The hospital was well equipped, and also offered additional training sessions every week.

Come what may, their plan was to spend a year there and save up as much money as possible. What would happen afterward remained an open question. "We didn't know if we'd like America," Helga says. In April 1956 they returned to Vienna, where they spent the rest of their lives. Why?

Although they had both studied English, they didn't speak it fluently when they arrived. Helga didn't much care but was soon able to make herself understood. To this day, she's fluent in English, although her Viennese mother tongue remains clearly audible. Hansi, however, felt hindered by not being able to fully express himself with his usual ease and levity. "I try to hide my linguistic incompetence with an understanding grunt, but sometimes my despair reveals itself," he wrote Pepi. "When I talk to patients, I formulate my questions in such a way that they can only be answered with a simple yes or no." He often feels like he's "in a glass box," watching people talk, but not understanding them, especially when they speak with any kind of accent. "When I meet a new person, it takes me nearly ten or fifteen minutes to get used to their unique tone." A month later, he felt better: "I understand ninety percent of what's said to me. (That doesn't apply to people who mumble, slur, or swallow their words.)" But even after all that, he never did manage to properly pronounce anything with *th* in it.

I had a similar experience when I was twenty and went off to study in England. I quickly discovered how tedious and exhausting it all was: formulating sentences before speaking them out loud; feeling so uncertain of how to use words you've read in actual conversation; people's facial expressions when they can't understand you; how difficult it is to explain more complicated trains of thought. "What I miss most, here in America, is my own personality," Hansi wrote in September. Emigration means so much more than just a change of scenery.

Hansi's correspondence with Pepi kept him connected to his homeland, and he wrote at least one long letter a week. When I ask my grandmother about Poughkeepsie yet again, she hands me a big bag full of aerograms, letters typed onto a single, postage-paid sheet of thin, light-blue paper that then folds up into itself, seals up as an envelope, and is addressed and sent by air mail.

Many of Hansi's letters are a linguistic mixture, and rereading them, I notice how quickly his English improved:

"*Everybody speaks English to me*, so when I think, sleep, and talk, I mix German and English expressions," he writes shortly after arrival. Little by little, the English parts become longer and increasingly error-free. He reports that he also reads novels from the hospital library. Language can't have been the real reason they returned to Vienna, I think.

Then what was it? Financially, they were doing better than ever before. They lived frugally. They bought and shared a used car with two other interns. Hansi's brother-in-law, Litzi's husband, taught him how to drive. In return, he helped build an addition to her one-story home on Long Island, for a new dining room. Hansi showed up to the driving test with his own car, which was common at the time. Shortly after the test started, the car stopped in its tracks. The other couple they shared it with had forgotten to refill the gas tank. A few weeks later, Hansi went back to take the test a second time and passed.

There is constant pressure to buy new things, Hansi writes. Therefore, many people are deep in debt. "It's like they just love having gift-giving orgies over here," he writes one June after Father's Day, when his cousin Litzi gave him a shirt ("despite the fact that I'm not even a dad"), and he frantically went out to get his own uncle a gift—aftershave—at the very last minute. But, by the same token, he was also fascinated by the technological innovations he was discovering, and was now able to write about them in English: "*Litzi got last week a new dish-washer. This is a machine in which you can put all your dishes and glasses then you close and after half an hour your dishes are clean and dry and you must only take them out."*

Were my grandparents lonely and socially isolated, as one sometimes hears immigrants say? Quite the contrary. It seems they could barely say no to all the invitations. Fellow doctors and hospital employees had them over, and they went to parties and the movies. One family that had to travel for several weeks even generously let them stay in their stately home while they were away. Helga and Hansi spent most of their time in the living room, listening to records.

Time and again they'd run into acquaintances from Vienna who had emigrated like them. They spent their free weekends in New York City with the family, who wanted to show them around town and help them integrate. They went to concerts, the theater, and museums, and they enjoyed lavish dinners for the Jewish holidays. Hansi appreciated his intelligent and attentive aunt, his engaged and family-oriented cousin, and his good-natured and amicable uncle. Helga's memories of Hansi's family are also very positive.

In July, Hansi writes Pepi that a friendly fellow Jewish doctor invited them to go swimming—at a "Jewish lake." "Poughkeepsie's Jews have bought their own lake. Everything here is separated. There isn't much mixing. People stay in their own little circles, with others of the same social background." Helga confirms it; she had found the degree of racial segregation, in particular, deeply disturbing. The staff of the hospital was mixed; their fellow interns included a black doctor, and her senior physician was black as well. On paper, New

York was one of the most progressive states when it came to anti-discrimination legislation. A government commission against discrimination at work had been introduced in 1945; from 1952 onward, people could sue for unequal treatment in public places; by 1954, segregation in schools had been declared illegal nationwide. Reality was rather different, Helga learned, when one of her black colleagues gave her a lift into the center of Poughkeepsie. Helga asked if he'd like to go shopping with her. He declined, saying that he couldn't be seen beside a white woman in public.

She was no less disturbed upon learning that an Austrian acquaintance who worked at the same hospital often wasn't invited when they were. Jewish doctors invited the Jewish couple, but not their non-Jewish friend. "I had had enough of that during the war," says Helga. So rigid, racist social conventions certainly played a major role in their decision to return to Europe.

But why didn't they just go to New York City, a more open-minded metropolis? "New York sure is exciting," Hansi wrote Pepi in July. "Its incredible dynamism and sheer diversity of races gives the whole place a certain fairytale feeling. Never have I seen such a vibrant city, so teeming with life. Riding the subway and seeing so many different faces is itself a form of entertainment." They would have been able to get a job there as well. Depending on the state, there were different requirements that they would have needed to meet, but they definitely could have gotten a license to practice medicine.

Well, says Helga, they still had family in Vienna—Pepi above all.

"Dear father," Hansi began each of his letters. Five years earlier, on January 24, 1950, the two had signed an adoption agreement. "Completed between Dr. Josef Feldner, MD, b. May 1, 1887 in Vienna, on the one hand, and Hans Bustin, his foster son, b. Oct. 18, 1925 in Vienna, on the other. Dr. Josef Feldner adopts Hans Bustin as his child, and assumes all duties which, according to law, foster parents pledge to provide for their adoptive children, with the exception of a pension, and grants the foster child all rights entitled by law, with the exception of pension. Hans Bustin accepts this request and promises to recognize Dr. Josef Feldner as his adoptive father and to fulfill all obligations of an adopted son, with the exception of any pension-related obligations. Henceforth, Hans Bustin shall go by the name Hans Feldner-Bustin."

Although Pepi's answers to Hansi's letters haven't been preserved, Hansi's texts bring the relationship of the two to life for me. I notice that my grandfather was clearly writing to someone he was used to interacting with on a daily basis. He skips segues, hops from subject to subject, dispenses with courtesy phrases, and expresses concern for everyday matters—kitchen renovations, cold winter weather, distant relatives' personalities and quirks. His tone is respectful yet familiar. A few months before Hansi's departure, Pepi published his book on pediatrics, and Hansi got as wound up as Pepi must have when he was invited to give a lecture. Pepi was shy and wanted little to do with the academic world.

Hansi repeatedly encourages him to present his theories, mentions that he's reread this or that passage from the book and finds it particularly well done, and uses terms he picked up from Pepi. Hansi concludes almost every letter with an admonition that his father be careful to eat enough and not work too much. Several times Hansi reminds Pepi to send his measurements, so he can buy him shirts and shoes in the US. And, over and over, he asks Pepi if he needs money. Obviously Pepi never replied to such questions, so Hansi simply sent small amounts and little gifts here and there back to Vienna, unsolicited.

Hansi writes that they will have a lot to tell one another when they finally see each other again. He emphasizes details above all: "People don't really place much value in having their children have proper posture," he says after visiting friends. "Kids roll around rather creatively all over the floor, striking picturesque poses, and even grown-ups sometimes sit on the floor." And people's relationship to money is completely different from what he's used to back home: "There is no sentimentality in business here," he writes. "It sounds paradoxical, but people here donate huge sums of money to charity, for truly charitable work, but they don't spare anyone a dime when it comes to business matters." He also finds how people deal with death rather different here: "Most people are embalmed and made up to look incredibly elegant. They're often more beautiful as corpses than they ever were before."

The more time passes, the more frequently Hansi writes how much he misses Pepi, especially their evening talks.

Toward the end of the summer, his mood finally plummets. "Dear Father, I miss you so much. We're now halfway through our time here, but it's a bit like strudel layers, a never-ending swirl, time just isn't moving. The months drag on, and I'd like it to be December, or January, with our day of departure clearly in sight." He even thinks about leaving early, but decides against it, because he still wants to improve his English.

Hansi and Helga ultimately decided to return to Vienna after their internship was over. Hansi hesitated for months before finally telling his aunt. Perhaps, he wonders, it might have been wiser to tell everyone, from day one, that their stay would eventually come to an end, because the reaction of those around him was unanimous: "Everybody says we're crazy to leave. Doctors make such a good living. The latter is true. But living well is no small task in this country. And besides, you can quickly take money for granted."

Only in October did Hansi muster the courage to tell his family about their departure that March. The announcement shook his aunt so much that he followed up with a six-page letter a few days later. "I want to tell you about me, about Pepi and me. He's now sixty-nine, and he's been in my life for over thirteen years. I've never talked much about my emotional life, my relationships, and what he means to me, since I find the subject difficult to broach. But I have no inhibitions about telling you, because I know how sympathetic you can be, how understanding. People generally expect me to be grateful to him for what he's done for me, and it's only logical that this sense of gratitude shapes my decisions and actions. But gratitude is only a tiny part of what I feel for him. He was, and still is, a fatherly friend to me, the person who tried to replace both of my parents during a very difficult time, and to the extent that anyone could ever succeed at all in accomplishing such an impossible task, he succeeded. He succeeded so well that I now cling to him with a childlike love and adoration. His well-being factors into all my considerations, and I must confess, I don't feel well here." He mentions two acquaintances whose parents, the same age as Pepi, recently and quite unexpectedly died. Pepi was in good health, but the moment he needed Hansi's presence could come at any time—"and the thought of being so helplessly far away is unbearable." "He never once made the slightest hint that I should come back, but we always had an unspoken agreement that we wanted to live together. . . . Both of us only feel well when we're within arm's reach of each other. When I go back to Vienna next March, I'm not going to pay a debt of gratitude, I'm going because I have a deep-seated personal need to see him happy."

He had weighed it carefully: "As for you, I know you observe my life with the eyes of a mother, that you're worried sick, and the last thing I'd ever want is to hurt your feelings." But she was well cared for by her family, while Pepi, his father, was living all alone in Vienna. Although Pepi had offered to move to the States, Hansi didn't think it advisable. Furthermore, Helga also felt obliged to be closer to her family, which was now firmly anchored in Vienna again. That's why Hansi felt he was doing the right thing.

I hold this letter in my hands a few weeks before my own departure from New York. I am with Litzi, who is now ninety-two and still lives in her cottage out on Long Island. Her TV is in the sunroom that, once upon a time, my grandfather helped build. I suspect it still looks almost exactly as it did back then. The brown, finely carved sideboard, the round dining table, the living room wallpaper—the only difference I see is the many photos on the walls, shelves, and atop the piano, showing that Litzi has two grandchildren and three great-grandchildren. She's lost some of her independence in recent years, which is why her daughter is scouring the house for documents that might interest me. She finds the "Holland-America Line Contract of Carriage," which allowed Hansi's Aunt Frieda and her husband to flee to the United States in November 1939; a letter from an American Jewish aid organization, which in September 1941 sought in vain for a visa for Frieda's older sister, Sophie; the naturalization certificates of Litzi and her parents, issued in December 1945; an invitation to the wedding of Hansi and Litzi's cousin Ilse in London in July 1951. And Hansi's long letter to his Aunt Frieda.

This letter is an eye-opener for me. My grandfather was someone who didn't talk much about his feelings. A few years after his death, we cleared out his old basement workshop. There, where his workbench had been, we discovered a depression under the linoleum in the floor, a spot so large that an adult could lie down in it. It was connected to a ventilation pipe that led to the outside. Never before had any of us noticed it. The fear of persecution never left Hansi. He suffered from insomnia, and there were days when he just wanted to be left alone. His purposeful pessimism—"if you don't have any expectations, you can't be disappointed"—set him apart from Pepi, who was for the most part confident and cheerful. I had only been able to imagine how close they truly were, how much they really loved each other, until I discovered that letter.

In the spring of 1973, seventeen years after Hansi and Helga returned from the States, Pepi fell and broke his femur. He was eighty-six years old. Pepi had always been suspicious of other doctors when it came to his own health, and at the hospital, he refused to let the staff look after him. Hansi took care of him and spent nights there. "When he was sick he'd usually just withdraw from his surroundings, and wouldn't eat for days, until his condition stabilized and passed on its own," Hansi writes. "Pepi had a deeply rooted conviction that every disease has a beginning, a middle, and an end, and that this natural course can easily be disturbed by a doctor's intervention. He also fully accepted that the end result of such a natural course of events could well be death." Pepi's last apartment was on the ground floor of my grandparents' house in the nineteenth district. Its large windows reached all the way to the floor, so he could look directly out into the courtyard greenery. Hansi made a wooden ramp so he could push Pepi's bed into the garden. It was a mild spring when Pepi died.

In his will, Pepi bequeathed to Hansi his few possessions, and wished that all his scientific work be left to his adoptive son. His corpse was to be cremated, with no one but the funeral parlor staff present. No music, no speech, "since the burial attendant couldn't possibly be interested," and no printed announcement. "My relatives and acquaintances shall be informed of my death as their paths happen to cross, in person." Hansi did not respect Pepi's last will. The entire family was present as Pepi's remains were placed in the Feldner family tomb near Villach. Yet Hansi probably did fulfill Pepi's most important wish: "I consider my son the ideal representative of my intellectual potential, and I am convinced that, through him, I shall continue to exist."

RETURN TO VIENNA

In the summer of 2015, I take the train back to New York from the suburbs where Litzi lives. As I take one last walk down the blocks between the station and the building where I live, in a room that's now nearly emptied out, I wonder whether I've been looking at my problem with New York from the wrong angle. For a long time, I thought I wanted to go back to Vienna because I felt lonely. But what if I felt lonely because I wanted to go back to Vienna? Had a part of me, perhaps unconsciously, realized long ago how very privileged I was to even have a home where I felt welcome? Maybe that's why I hadn't put much effort into creating a new network, a circle of friends, a substitute for my family. I had just drifted and found only a few deeper relationships that seemed as if they might last.

I met many people in New York who lived there because there was no space for them where they had come from. My own great aunt. The Chinese journalist who couldn't freely practice her profession back home. The vegetable vendor from Bangladesh and the cleaning lady from Ecuador who were supporting their families back home. My friend from Italy who needed some distance from a difficult relationship. The Pilates coach from Spain who just wanted a chance to work. My colleague from Georgia who was a toddler when her family fled from war. My acquaintance from a small town in Florida, where he'd faced discrimination because of his homosexuality. That wasn't my story. I had come here for adventure, but now I yearned for the comfort of those family dinners.

*

By the winter of 1955, Hansi's letters to Pepi focused mainly on his return journey. My grandparents have saved enough to buy a car in Vienna, a used Volkswagen. Hansi also hopes to get a new bed. And would they all share an apartment? Hansi hopes he and Helga might move in with Pepi on Neubaugasse. "I know the most natural thing would be to grow up, move out, get an apartment of our own, and bring children into the world," Hansi writes Pepi. "But I have no such ambitions. I don't want to move away from you (because then I might as well just stay in America), nor do I aspire to have my own household and children."

At the end of March 1956, they board a ship bound for Cherbourg. The trip back is as stormy as the outbound journey had been. Helga is constantly nauseous. It's not just seasickness.

*

My grandparents first moved into their own apartment when Helga was already pregnant with her second child, my mother. They had lived with her parents after their first son was born. Years later—after my uncle, their fourth and

Pepi, a relative, and Hansi, 1950s.

final child, was born—they found a larger apartment in the nineteenth district. The family of six moved in on the second floor. When an apartment was vacated on the ground floor, Hansi set it up for Pepi. The two of them had breakfast together every morning.

Hansi returned to America twice, for a few months each time, because of the better earning potential there. While posted at a private clinic with all the latest technology, he discovered a new device that recorded electrical activity in the brain. Electroencephalography is used in neurology to diagnose epilepsy and other such conditions. Hansi bought an EEG device and shipped it to Austria. After Pepi moved out of Neubaugasse, Hansi converted his former hiding place into a doctor's office and exam room in which he saw patients. Soon business was so good that he gave up his job at the city-run clinic. He had always said he was allergic to supervisors; Helga, however, enjoyed working at the hospital until the day she retired.

Hansi and Helga worked while Hertha, Helga's mother, took care of the four children. She would pick them up from school by car, always impeccably dressed in a skirt with matching jacket, hat, and pumps. She set her white leather clutch on the back seat. It was always full of little chocolates and cream-filled bunnies for the children to enjoy.

At lunch, my great-grandmother taught her grandchildren proper manners. One's upper arms must be close enough to the torso to pinch a book in the space between. Children weren't to speak until spoken to. Pepi also came for lunch. In the wintertime, he would always bring roasted chestnuts and set them on the table before the meal. My mother remembers the kids wanting to eat them right away, but Hertha insisted they be distributed only after the main course. Each day, Pepi followed their banter in silence.

Pepi's relationship to Helga and her parents remained fairly distant; their personalities were quite different. Helga had no choice but to accept Pepi's presence. He and Hansi were symbiotic, she says. Pepi was there for every holiday, usually kept quiet, and never interfered. Only now have I come across the notes he took on the four grandchildren's development over the years. When asked, "What did you do in kindergarten today?" my uncle said, "went poopie." My mother asked Pepi if he had a wife, mother, or father, and was shocked when he said no. Didn't that make him sad? Some of Pepi's notes are hurtful in their severity. He often comes to extreme conclusions, calling people "lying," "gross," or "selfish." I doubt such judgments were meant for anyone's eyes but his.

As my mother and her siblings grew up, Hertha's rules relaxed a bit. She would give them money and became their go-to person for things they would rather not discuss with their parents. When Hertha and Paul traveled, they'd leave their apartment to their grandchildren. Hertha survived her husband by more than twenty years. My mother says her grandfather had a pleasant scent of cigars and aftershave. He worked as a police-department doctor until retirement, and he was eventually granted the honorary title of *Hofrat*, the equivalent of privy councilor. He could often be seen taking his dachshund, Pitzi, for walks. He was a nervous, anxious, sentimental man. He insisted on blessing family members before important events, be it a school exam or air travel. He did so according to Old Testament tradition, laying his hands on their heads and reciting the priestly blessing. "May the Lord bless you and keep you, and let his face shine unto you and be gracious to you. May the Lord lift up His face unto you and give you peace." When he couldn't do it in person, he'd call and demand that the telephone receiver be held over the intended beneficiary's head.

I was eight years old when my great-grandmother died in 1997. I remember seeing her sitting in bed, frail, nearly blind. Nevertheless, her lips were red and her hair perfectly coiffed. Her white leather clutch was always next to her on the bed.

*

After Pepi's death in 1973, the family suggested having a tree planted for him along the Avenue of the Righteous at the Yad Vashem Holocaust Memorial in Jerusalem. An Israeli commission awards the title "Righteous Among the Nations" to those who rescued Jews under Nazi persecution. To this day, Pepi is not one of them. He wouldn't have wanted that under any circumstances, Hansi said—he found such sentimental gestures offensive. To Pepi, what he had done was self-evident. Why should he be honored for not doing the wrong thing?

For a long time, this struck me as incomprehensible. How could a monument be bad if it moved people to see Pepi as a role model and emulate his behavior? I had always listened in as members of our extended family were ranked according to whether they would hide us. My grandmother's longtime medical secretary? Absolutely. My cousins' former nanny? Probably not. My classmate's parents? Maybe. Many of Pepi's traits were inherited by the family. The art of listening and questioning, for example: Pepi taught Hansi, who passed it on to my mother, who used it on me. If someone annoyed or offended me, she would let me tell her all about it and ask if I could guess why they might have done what they did. Today I consider listening to people the most strenuous aspect of my job as a journalist: I have to pay close attention to what people say, suss out whether they're saying it merely because they think it's what I want to hear, and then formulate my next question.

Pepi's sheer courage and recklessness often make such family lore sound like a bunch of adventure stories, but I'm a long way from all that. Would I be capable of standing up against a seemingly invincible, perilous power? I don't know.

My high school hallways had glass fire doors. Most of the time, they were held open by a strong magnet, so there was an empty triangle between the door frame, door, and wall. During break one day, when my classmates and I were ten or eleven, we came upon a closed fire door. One of us came up with the idea of opening the door and then having one of us squeeze into that triangle. The girl chosen was someone I didn't like because, in gym class a few months before, she had told everyone not to pass the ball to me. From a sports perspective, it was completely justified, but it devastated me.

One of us pushed the girl to the other side of the glass door. Then four or five others, including me, leaned against the door. Everyone laughed, including the trapped girl, who used both arms to brace herself against the door. She played along, perhaps grateful for the attention. Clearly, she wasn't comfortable; her laugh had the high pitch of despair. But as soon as the magnet clicked shut, she sank to the floor and started to cry. Her right arm suddenly hung limp. A teacher rushed over to free her.

That afternoon, I reflected on what had happened. I had a guilty conscience and burst into tears in front of my mother. She handed me the phone. The girl seemed to be happy about my call. I stammered out an apology. She had sprained her shoulder joint, but it didn't hurt that much anymore. Then she asked me what she had missed in math class. We became friends, did our homework together during lunch break, and passed the ball to one another in gym class. After completing high school, I lost track of her.

That was almost twenty years ago, and yet I can still see the expression on her face as she strained against the glass door. Locking her up, shutting her in had been a game—a game that, all of a sudden, had real consequences when she sank to the floor, cradling her injured shoulder. What would have happened, I wonder, if our game had ended as we had expected, culminating not in injury but in her mutually agreed-upon liberation? Maybe I wouldn't have realized that I had done something wrong, that I had been part of a group that overpowered an individual and didn't ask for consent. The consequences of my actions would have remained invisible, abstract.

According to this logic, a lot of people during the Nazi era would have felt compelled to join the resistance, especially those with a lot of persecuted friends. They experienced the consequences of their non-action more clearly than anyone else. This applies to Pepi, who knew my grandfather's family before 1938—and yet at the same time, such reasoning falls short. What about those who were all too happy to get rid of their competitors, their neighbors—no matter how close they'd been before? No, Pepi did something different: he felt responsible. Taking responsibility is a decision. Someone who takes responsibility takes action. Pepi decided he had a role to play in my grandfather's life.

A tree in Jerusalem can't even begin to explain all that. Pepi's legacy is alive. He has sixteen descendants, and his roots run deep in each of us.

*

The day of my master's degree graduation ceremony in May 2013 is muggy. Several streets around the university are closed to accommodate the ten thousand expected visitors. I've borrowed the light-blue gown and matching cap from an alum, with just one little oversight: the gowns come in different sizes, and my generous predecessor is at least a foot taller.

We sit on the metal bleachers and cheer when the video camera projecting our class onto the big screen pans by us. I wonder if this sense of belonging, something everyone here clearly seems to feel, actually exists. Sure, I'm *experiencing* an adventure, but am I really *part of it?* The light-blue, oversized gown sticks to the back of my knees.

I find my parents and grandmother again in one of the huge party tents. Helga, eighty-four at the time, had announced that she wouldn't miss it for the world, and flew over. The way she said it almost sounded like a threat: no one can keep me from coming. A few months earlier, I had

Helga and Anna, New York, May 22, 2013.

produced a piece about my trip to Poughkeepsie for the university's broadcast reporting workshop. Now some of my curious classmates wander over and want to meet my grandmother. The professor introduces himself to her too.

That weekend, just before Helga returns to Vienna, we take our last daytrip together in New York. It's just a forty-five minute ride to Litzi's on the Long Island Railroad. She picks us up from the station by car. It's the last time I get to see the ninety-year-old behind the wheel.

We sit in the sunroom of her little one-story cottage and eat cake. The conversation meanders here and there, and Litzi asks after each family member. When she pronounces a name, she enunciates every syllable, sounding overly respectful. She usually still puts a "dear" in front, too. No matter what Helga says in response, Litzi is invariably enthusiastic. "He's having a hard time at school . . . " "You don't say—well, I'm sure he'll do a great job!" Helga gives Litzi health tips, and she graciously nods after each recommendation.

I'm so distracted by my own insecurities that I hardly even listen. I had recently agreed to go to Berlin for an internship, but now I'm wondering whether I'd actually rather stay in New York. One year wasn't enough. Maybe that's how my grandparents felt when they got here: eager but uncertain, curious as to whether this would be just another adventure or the start of a new life.

We take a taxi back to the train station. Litzi stands in her front yard and waves to us as we go. Helga looks exhausted. She's also clearly looking forward to Vienna, to her everyday life, to the family. I will miss her.

ANNA GOLDENBERG, born in 1989 in Vienna, studied psychology at the University of Cambridge and journalism at Columbia University. She worked at the Jewish newspaper *The Forward* in New York before returning to Vienna where she now writes as a freelance journalist.

ALTA L. PRICE translates from Italian and German, and was awarded the 2013 Gutekunst Prize. Her publications include work by Corrado Augias, Dana Grigorcea, Jürgen Holstein, and Martin Mosebach.

ACKNOWLEDGMENTS

My thanks go to the publishing team at Paul Zsolnay Verlag in Vienna, and Herbert Ohrlinger in particular, for believing in this project. Thanks to Fanny Esterházy for the gentle editing. I'm much obliged to Michael Z. Wise and his team at New Vessel Press for bringing my family's story (back) to the US, and to Alta L. Price for her thoughtful translation.

This book would never have been possible were it not for countless long conversations with my grandmother, Helga Feldner-Bustin. Thank you for letting me tell your story.

Encouraging feedback and suggestions that improved numerous versions of this manuscript were generously provided by Nina Brnada, Georg Goldenberg, and Uschi Korda.

"Why don't you write a book about it?" Florian Klenk asked after my article "The Diary of Hansi Busztin" appeared in *Falter* 17/2015. Thanks for the excellent encouragement!

I thank Herwig Czech, Jutta Fuchshuber, Dieter Hecht, Michaela Raggam-Blesch, Oliver Rathkolb, Barbara Sauer, Fritz Trümpi, Brigitte Ungar-Klein, and Maria von der Heydt for answering my history-related questions. Thanks also to Hubert Deutsch (1925–2018), Ilse Feldstein, Liese Scheiderbauer, and Litzi Small for telling me stories from your own past.

Many thanks to Georg and Lorle Lukeschitsch, who

showed me Pepi's grave in Carinthia; Morgan Mansour, who drove me to Vassar Brothers Hospital in Poughkeepsie; Maria Asperger Felder, who sent me documents from the estate of Hans Asperger; Renate Mercsanits, who granted me access to the Archives of GRG3, the secondary school on Radetzkystrasse; Lynda Savyon, who retrieved family documents for me in the United States; and the editors of *ZEITmagazin*, who made our trip to Theresienstadt possible and published my report *"Das Leben danach"* ("Life Afterward") in *ZEITmagazin* 51/2013. Thanks also to cousin Laura, for being there with me.

I am deeply grateful to my friends, who checked in to see how I was doing ("May I also ask about the book?"), patiently listened to my replies, and showed me how healthy a little distraction can be. The *chaverim* at Hashomer Hatzair Ken Wien were particularly helpful, as was my *kvutza*, Beit-Kama; Svenja Esins, Alexander Glasner, and Sarah Hale, who have traveled far and wide for our friendship; Agnes and Sophie Langer, who have been there for me since 1989; Adam Langer, Maia Efrem Margolies, and Frauke Steffens, as well as Trudy Jeremias and her regulars at the *Stammtisch*, who make it a joy for me to think back to my time in New York; and all my journalist colleagues who stood at the ready, offering inspiring conversation at all hours.

Without the support of my family, this book would never have come into existence. I didn't realize how much our family ties meant to me until I missed them so much. Thanks for all the dinners.

ARCHIVAL SOURCES AND REFERENCES

Archiv IKG Wien (Vienna JC Archives). Jerusalem holdings, emigration forms: A/W 2589.8—Bustyn, Moritz; A/W 2590,84—Gusowsky and Bustin.

Asperger, Hans. "Dr. Josef Feldner–75 Jahre," in Hans Asperger and Hans Redl (eds.), *Heilpädagogik. Beiblatt der Zeitschrift »Erziehung und Unterricht«.* Vienna, 1962, 56–58.

Beckermann, Ruth (ed.). *Die Mazzesinsel. Juden in der Wiener Leopoldstadt 1918 bis 1938.* Vienna: Löcker, 1984.

Benz, Wolfgang. *Theresienstadt. Eine Geschichte von Täuschung und Vernichtung.* Munich: Beck, 2013.

Documentation Centre of the Austrian Resistance (DÖW). Municipal Buildings Database, Dr. Ing. Paul Pollak, eviction decree (Margareten neighborhood), eviction letter.

―――. Gestapo Tagesrapporte, daily reports, June 5–7, 1942: 7.

Exenberger, Herbert, Johann Koss, and Brigitte Ungar-Klein. *Kündigungsgrund Nichtarier. Die Vertreibung jüdischer Mieter aus den Wiener Gemeindebauten in den Jahren 1938–1939.* Vienna: Picus, 1996.

Fein, Erich, and Karl Flanner. *Rot-weiss-rot in Buchenwald.* Vienna: Europaverlag, 1987.

Frank, Anne: Diary. *The Diary of a Young Girl.* Tr. Susan Massotty. New York: Penguin, 2010.

Gibs, Helga. *Leopoldstadt. Kleine Welt am grossen Strom.* Vienna: Mohl, 1997.

Hecht, Dieter J., Eleonore Lappin-Eppel, and Michaela Raggam-Blesch. *Topographie der Shoah. Gedächtnisorte des zerstörten jüdischen Wien.* Vienna: Mandelbaum, 2015.

Jou, Chin. "Neither Welcomed, Nor Refused: Race and Restaurants in Postwar New York City," in *Journal of Urban History* 40.2 (March 2014): 232–251.

Klamper, Elisabeth. "Die Situation der jüdischen Bevölkerung in Wien von Ausbruch bis Ende des Krieges," in Dokumentationsarchiv des österreichischen Widerstandes (ed.), *Erzählte Geschichte, Band 3: Jüdische Schicksale*. Vienna: DÖW, 1993: 164–176.

Klüger, Ruth. *Still Alive: A Holocaust Girlhood Remembered*. New York: Feminist Press, 2003.

Köstner, Christina, and Klaus Voigt (eds.). *Österreichisches Exil in Italien 1938–1945*. Vienna: Mandelbaum, 2009.

Loewy, Hanno, and Gerhard Milchram (eds.). *Hast Du meine Alpen gesehen? Eine jüdische Beziehungsgeschichte*. Hohenems: Bucher, 2009.

Löw, Andrea, Doris L. Bergen, and Anna Hájková (eds.). *Alltag im Holocaust. Jüdisches Leben im Grossdeutschen Reich 1941–1945*. Munich: Oldenbourg, 2013.

Militär-Wissenschaftlicher Verein. *Jahresbericht über die k. k. Militär- Erziehungs- und Bildungs-Anstalten dann über die Officiers Töchter-Erziehungs-Institute*. Vienna: k. k. Hof- und Staatsdruckerei, 1884.

Österreichisches Staatsarchiv (Austrian State Archives). Compensation and Restitution Division, Property Transaction Office, Statistics, Act 10505.

———. Compensation and Restitution Division, Property Transaction Office, Danube Adjustment, Carton 1235.

———. Compensation and Restitution Division, Property Declarations, AT-OeStA/AdR

E-uReang VVSt VA, Letter P 2408, Pollak, Paul.

———. Nazi-era Civil records, Vienna Regional staff registry ("Gauakten"), AT-OeStA / CoR ZNsZ GA. Press and Information Service of the City of Vienna: Historical overview of the city-hall correspondence, entry for April 1945, www. wien.gv.at/rk/historisch/1945/april.html.

Rabinovici, Doron. *Instanzen der Ohnmacht. Wien 1938 bis 1945. Der Weg zum Judenrat.* Frankfurt am Main: Jüdischer, 2000.

Schuschnigg, Kurt. Last broadcast address as Austrian Chancellor, March 11, 1938. Österreichischen Mediathek (Austrian Media Library) file, www.mediathek.at.

Serloth, Barbara. *Von Opfern, Tätern und jenen dazwischen. Wie Antisemitismus die Zweite Republik mitbegründete.* Vienna: Mandelbaum, 2016.

Tálos, Emmerich. *Das austrofaschistische Herrschaftssystem. Österreich 1933 bis 1938.* Berlin: Lit, 2013.

Tolts, Mark: "Population and Migration: Migration since World War I," in the YIVO Encyclopedia of Jews in Eastern Europe, www.yivoencyclopedia.org.

United States Holocaust Memorial Museum: "German Jewish Refugees, 1933–1939," in the online Holocaust Encyclopedia, www.ushmm.org.

Walter, Michael. *Hitler in der Oper. Deutsches Musikleben 1919 bis 1945.* Stuttgart: J.B. Metzler, 2000.

Weinzierl, Erika. *Zu wenig Gerechte. Österreicher und Judenverfolgung 1938 bis 1945.* Graz: Syria, 1997 (4th ed.).

Wiener Stadt- und Landesarchiv (Municipal and Provincial Archives of Vienna). File MA 208, A36 – Victims' Welfare Acts-Compensation ("E"): Dr. Hans Feldner-Busztin.

———. File MA 208, A36–Victims' Welfare Acts-Compensation ("E"): Dr. Helga Feldner-Busztin.

THE DRIVE
BY YAIR ASSULIN

This searing novel tells the journey of a young Israeli soldier at the breaking point, unable to continue carrying out his military service, yet terrified of the consequences of leaving the army. As the soldier and his father embark on a lengthy drive to meet with a military psychiatrist, Yair Assulin penetrates the torn world of the hero, whose journey is not just that of a young man facing a crucial dilemma, but a tour of the soul and depths of Israeli society and of those everywhere who resist regimentation and violence.

VILLA OF DELIRIUM
BY ADRIEN GOETZ

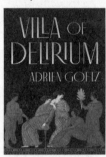

Along the French Riviera, an illustrious family in thrall to classical antiquity builds a fabulous villa—a replica of a Greek palace, complete with marble columns, furniture of exotic woods and frescoes depicting mythological gods. The Reinachs—related to other wealthy Jews like the Rothschilds and the Ephrussis—attempt in the early 1900s to recreate "a pure beauty" lost to modernity and fill it with the pursuit of pleasure and knowledge. This is a Greek epic for the modern era.

AND THE BRIDE CLOSED THE DOOR
BY RONIT MATALON

A young bride shuts herself up in a bedroom on her wedding day, refusing to get married. In this moving and humorous look at contemporary Israel and the chaotic ups and downs of love everywhere, her family gathers outside the locked door, not knowing what to do. The only communication they receive from behind the door are scribbled notes, one of them a cryptic poem about a prodigal daughter returning home. The harder they try to reach the defiant woman, the more the despairing groom is convinced that her refusal should be respected. But what, exactly, ought to be respected? Is this merely a case of cold feet?

ANIMAL INTERNET
BY ALEXANDER PSCHERA

Some 50,000 creatures around the globe—including whales, leopards, flamingoes, bats and snails—are being equipped with digital tracking devices. The data gathered and studied by major scientific institutes about their behavior will warn us about tsunamis, earthquakes and volcanic eruptions, but also radically transform our relationship to the natural world. Contrary to pessimistic fears, author Alexander Pschera sees the Internet as creating a historic opportunity for a new dialogue between man and nature.

EXPOSED
BY JEAN-PHILIPPE BLONDEL

A dangerous intimacy emerges between a French teacher and a former student who has achieved art world celebrity. The painting of a portrait upturns both their lives. Jean-Philippe Blondel, author of the bestselling novel *The 6:41 to Paris,* evokes an intimacy of dangerous intensity in a stunning tale about aging, regret and moving ahead into the future.

THE 6:41 TO PARIS
BY JEAN-PHILIPPE BLONDEL

Cécile, a stylish 47-year-old, has spent the weekend visiting her parents outside Paris. By Monday morning, she's exhausted. These trips back home are stressful and she settles into a train compartment with an empty seat beside her. But it's soon occupied by a man she recognizes as Philippe Leduc, with whom she had a passionate affair that ended in her brutal humiliation 30 years ago. In the fraught hour and a half that ensues, Cécile and Philippe hurtle towards the French capital in a psychological thriller about the pain and promise of past romance.

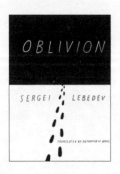

OBLIVION
BY SERGEI LEBEDEV

In one of the first 21st century Russian novels to probe the legacy of the Soviet prison camp system, a young man travels to the vast wastelands of the Far North to uncover the truth about a shadowy neighbor who saved his life, and whom he knows only as Grandfather II. Emerging from today's Russia, where the ills of the past are being forcefully erased from public memory, this masterful novel represents an epic literary attempt to rescue history from the brink of oblivion.

THE YEAR OF THE COMET
BY SERGEI LEBEDEV

A story of a Russian boyhood and coming of age as the Soviet Union is on the brink of collapse. Lebedev depicts a vast empire coming apart at the seams, transforming a very public moment into something tender and personal, and writes with stunning beauty and shattering insight about childhood and the growing consciousness of a boy in the world.

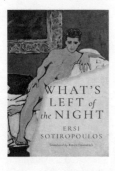

WHAT'S LEFT OF THE NIGHT
BY ERSI SOTIROPOULOS

Constantine Cavafy arrives in Paris in 1897 on a trip that will deeply shape his future and push him toward his poetic inclination. With this lyrical novel, tinged with an hallucinatory eroticism that unfolds over three unforgettable days, celebrated Greek author Ersi Sotiropoulos depicts Cavafy in the midst of a journey of self-discovery across a continent on the brink of massive change. A stunning portrait of a budding author—before he became C.P. Cavafy, one of the 20th century's greatest poets—that illuminates the complex relationship of art, life, and the erotic desires that trigger creativity.

THE EYE
BY PHILIPPE COSTAMAGNA

It's a rare and secret profession, comprising a few dozen people around the world equipped with a mysterious mixture of knowledge and innate sensibility. Summoned to Swiss bank vaults, Fifth Avenue apartments, and Tokyo storerooms, they are entrusted by collectors, dealers, and museums to decide if a coveted picture is real or fake and to determine if it was painted by Leonardo da Vinci or Raphael. *The Eye* lifts the veil on the rarified world of connoisseurs devoted to the authentication and discovery of Old Master artworks.

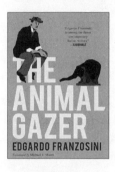

THE ANIMAL GAZER
BY EDGARDO FRANZOSINI

A hypnotic novel inspired by the strange and fascinating life of sculptor Rembrandt Bugatti, brother of the fabled automaker. Bugatti obsessively observes and sculpts the baboons, giraffes, and panthers in European zoos, finding empathy with their plight and identifying with their life in captivity. Rembrandt Bugatti's work, now being rediscovered, is displayed in major art museums around the world and routinely fetches large sums at auction. Edgardo Franzosini recreates the young artist's life with intense lyricism, passion, and sensitivity.

ALLMEN AND THE DRAGONFLIES
BY MARTIN SUTER

Johann Friedrich von Allmen has exhausted his family fortune by living in Old World grandeur despite present-day financial constraints. Forced to downscale, Allmen inhabits the garden house of his former Zurich estate, attended by his Guatemalan butler, Carlos. This is the first of a series of humorous, fast-paced detective novels devoted to a memorable gentleman thief. A thrilling art heist escapade infused with European high culture and luxury that doesn't shy away from the darker side of human nature.

THE MADELEINE PROJECT
BY CLARA BEAUDOUX

A young woman moves into a Paris apartment and discovers a storage room filled with the belongings of the previous owner, a certain Madeleine who died in her late nineties, and whose treasured possessions nobody seems to want. In an audacious act of journalism driven by personal curiosity and humane tenderness, Clara Beaudoux embarks on *The Madeleine Project*, documenting what she finds on Twitter with text and photographs, introducing the world to an unsung 20th century figure.

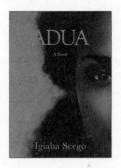

ADUA
BY IGIABA SCEGO

Adua, an immigrant from Somalia to Italy, has lived in Rome for nearly forty years. She came seeking freedom from a strict father and an oppressive regime, but her dreams of film stardom ended in shame. Now that the civil war in Somalia is over, her homeland calls her. She must decide whether to return and reclaim her inheritance, but also how to take charge of her own story and build a future.

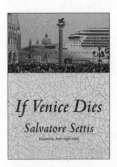

IF VENICE DIES
BY SALVATORE SETTIS

Internationally renowned art historian Salvatore Settis ignites a new debate about the Pearl of the Adriatic and cultural patrimony at large. In this fiery blend of history and cultural analysis, Settis argues that "hit-and-run" visitors are turning Venice and other landmark urban settings into shopping malls and theme parks. This is a passionate plea to secure the soul of Venice, written with consummate authority, wide-ranging erudition and élan.

THE MADONNA OF NOTRE DAME
BY ALEXIS RAGOUGNEAU

Fifty thousand people jam into Notre Dame Cathedral to celebrate the Feast of the Assumption. The next morning, a beautiful young woman clothed in white kneels at prayer in a cathedral side chapel. But when someone accidentally bumps against her, her body collapses. She has been murdered. This thrilling novel illuminates shadowy corners of the world's most famous cathedral, shedding light on good and evil with suspense, compassion and wry humor.

THE LAST WEYNFELDT
BY MARTIN SUTER

Adrian Weynfeldt is an art expert in an international auction house, a bachelor in his mid-fifties living in a grand Zurich apartment filled with costly paintings and antiques. Always correct and well-mannered, he's given up on love until one night—entirely out of character for him—Weynfeldt decides to take home a ravishing but unaccountable young woman and gets embroiled in an art forgery scheme that threatens his buttoned up existence. This refined page-turner moves behind elegant bourgeois facades into darker recesses of the heart.

MOVING THE PALACE
BY CHARIF MAJDALANI

A young Lebanese adventurer explores the wilds of Africa, encountering an eccentric English colonel in Sudan and enlisting in his service. In this lush chronicle of far-flung adventure, the military recruit crosses paths with a compatriot who has dismantled a sumptuous palace and is transporting it across the continent on a camel caravan. This is a captivating modern-day Odyssey in the tradition of Bruce Chatwin and Paul Theroux.

New Vessel Press

*To purchase these titles and for more information
please visit newvesselpress.com.*